NeoWhimsies

for beginners

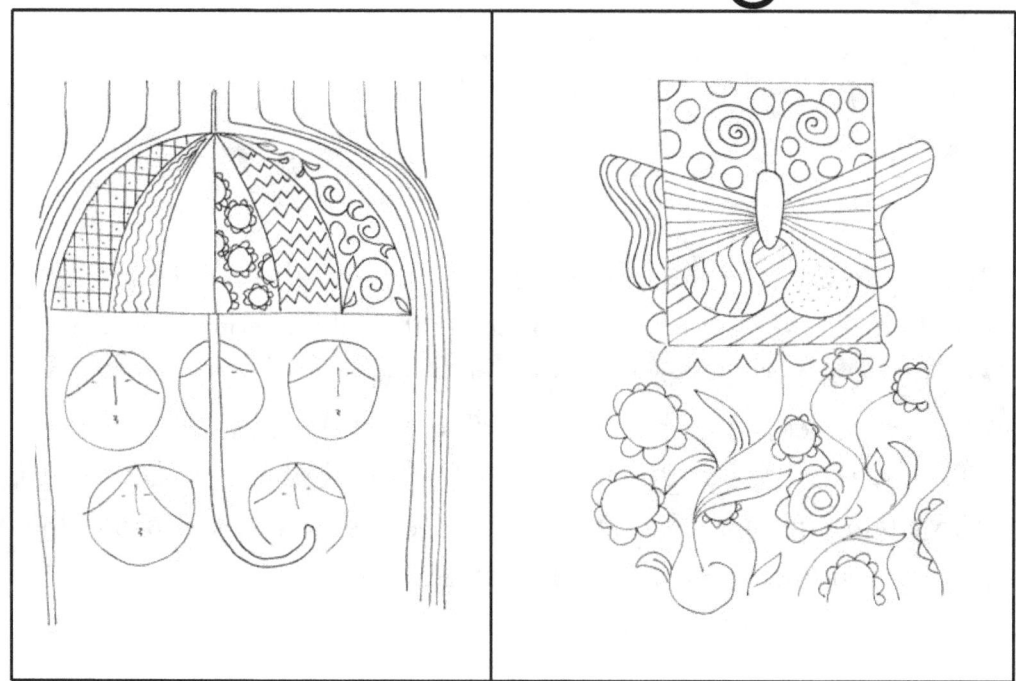

10 NEOPOPREALISM

ink drawing projects

ILLUSTRATED by SERGE E. MIKHAILOV

NeoPopRealism PRESS

NeoPopRealism ink drawings consist out of the sections, filled with different kinds of the repetitive patterns. It could be complicated ornaments or just zig-zag, or the small and simple flowers. . . Artist divides a piece of paper or object into the sections. And then, he fills these sections with different repetitive patterns. NeoPopRealism drawing is flat. Drawing of NeoPopRealism images is like game, because when you chose the next pattern, you use your intuition and imagination.

A book *"NeoWhimsies for Beginners: 10 NeoPopRealism Ink Drawing Projects"* by NeoPopRealism PRESS with illustrations by Serge E. Mikhailov invites you to learn how to draw the imaginative and whimsical ink images - NeoWhimsies. Albert Einstein said, "Imagination is more important than knowledge. For knowledge is limited, whereas imagination embraces the entire world, stimulating progress, giving birth to evolution. It is, strictly speaking, a real factor in scientific research."

The common use of the term 'Imagination' in arts is for the process of drawing new images that have not been previously experienced with the help of what has been seen before or at least only partially or in different combinations.

An illustrator of this book, Serge E. Mikhailov confessed that for him imagination is equal to memory and that he can "imagine" only things that he saw. Unfortunately, majority of people have the lack of imagination. However, this book is a try to teach the readers how to unlock their imagination and discover new dimension in arts. We hope it will be your step forward as it was a first step for Serge E. Mikhailov.

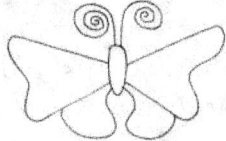

NeoWhimsies

for beginners

10 NeoPopRealism ink drawing projects

ILUSTRATED by Serge E. Mikhailov
NeoPopRealism PRESS

First published in 2012 by NeoPopRealism PRESS
PO BOX 366
New York, NY 10013

NeopoprealismPress@mail.com

"NeoWhimsies for Beginners: 10 NeoPopRealism Ink Drawing *Projects*" by NeoPopRealism PRESS
Illustrations by Serge E. Mikhailov

Published in the United States of America
Language: English

ISBN-13: 978-0615645087
ISBN-10: 0615645089

12 13 14 15 16   10 9 8 7 6 5 4 3 2 1

This book teaches how to draw NeoWhimsies - the NeoPopRealism ink images for beginners.

www.neopoprealism.org

CONTENT

INTRODUCTION

$\mathcal{N}$eoPopRealism art style including ink drawing concept was created by artist Nadia Russ in 1989.

It was an experiment. She was trying to connect to the Universe and let the Universe use her as a conductor when she created her drawings. She didn't want to follow any other artists' achievements, she decided to create absolutely new art form, like Picasso (Cubism), Dali (Surrealism), Andy Warhol (Pop Art) and a few other worldwide known artists had done.

Nadia Russ took her ink pen and began to draw a flowing line, which turned into shapes, figures, often faces. Then, some sections (or all), which appeared, she filled with the repetitive patterns. She never uses eraser because if a mistake made, it disappears with the following repetitive patterns that balance the whole composition. Her work was unique, no one did anything like this before.

Later, January 4, 2003, Nadia Russ created a word NeoPopRealism and internationally announced new style of visual arts. Today, her artwork can be found in the private, corporate and museums' art collections worldwide. She lives in the U.S.

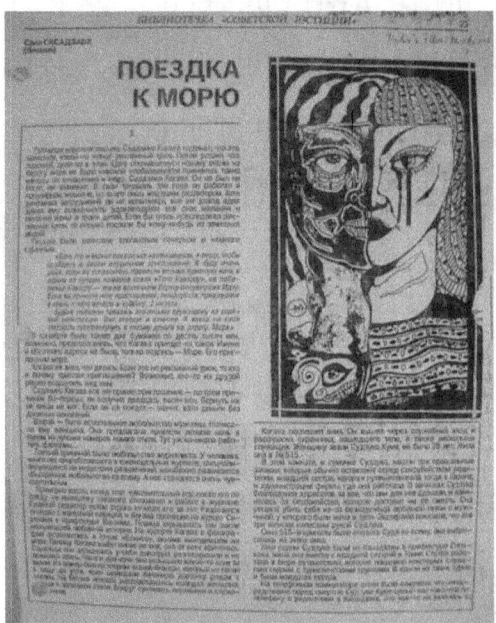

Nadia Russ illustrated a story by Saho Sasadzava for the *Russian Justice* Journal, 1992, Moscow, Russia

Get inspired

*O*ur first tip is for your success. Your mind is set in wide focus; it observes and takes what others would illuminate as irrelevant. The goals do not dominate the foreground of your mind. When you focus on your success, you fall into the trap of comparing yourself to other people, feeling envious. Instead, focus on getting better every day. Focus on excellence. Use your strengths for a bigger purpose beyond yourself. Focus on what you are giving instead of what you are getting, it makes every your step more rewarding and meaningful. The outstanding creative people have the following qualities: originality, Independence, persistence, self-confidence, non-conformity, orientation to achievement, skepticism, general knowledge, fluency, dynamism, holistic thinking, and sense of humor. If you do not have all of these qualities (yet), no problem. Now you know what you need to achieve to improve yourself as a creative person.

This book will teach you how to create the whimsical ink drawings. Strong positive emotions accompany the creative process. When you create, you experience a joy, an overflow of excited feelings or lasting sense of fulfillment.

Get your black ink pen *Foray Rolle Rollerball Medium 0.7 mm, Sharpie, or any other* and a piece of cardstock paper 8.5"x11". Cut it into two pieces - 5.5"x8.5" each. Now, you need one piece.

You would like to create something very unique and that's not always easy to do. Connect to the Universe and open your mind to the higher powers. Close your eyes for a moment. Imaging that your consciousness leaves your body and fly to the Space where there are no people but only super speed and super powers. Forget about your daily life experiences. No noise should disturb you except, possible, music. You are not you any more; you are a part of the Universe. . . Slowly open your eyes. Try not to look around, look only at your piece of a plain white paper. This is the beginning. . . Now draw. If you couldn't draw the Whimsies - simple NeoPopRealism images, then go to the next pages of this book. After you learn how to draw with the all offered tips and tricks, come back to this page again and let see what will happen.

Learn how to draw NeoWhimsies and you will be able to create more complicated, NeoPopRealism artwork and exhibit it in the art galleries.

Draw the Umbrellas

*T*he following pages will show you how to draw the NeoWhimsies Umbrellas.

This is how Serge E. Mikhailov creates his drawings:

Serge draws a line that creates the sections. Then he fills these sections with different repetitive patterns. Each Umbrella – NeoWhimsy – is different; each Whimsy carries the different meaning. The following visual instructions will teach you step-by-step how to create these Whimsies. They will lead you from the beginning to end of the drawing process. Every following image includes new detail(s). The final NeoWhimsies Umbrellas look like this:

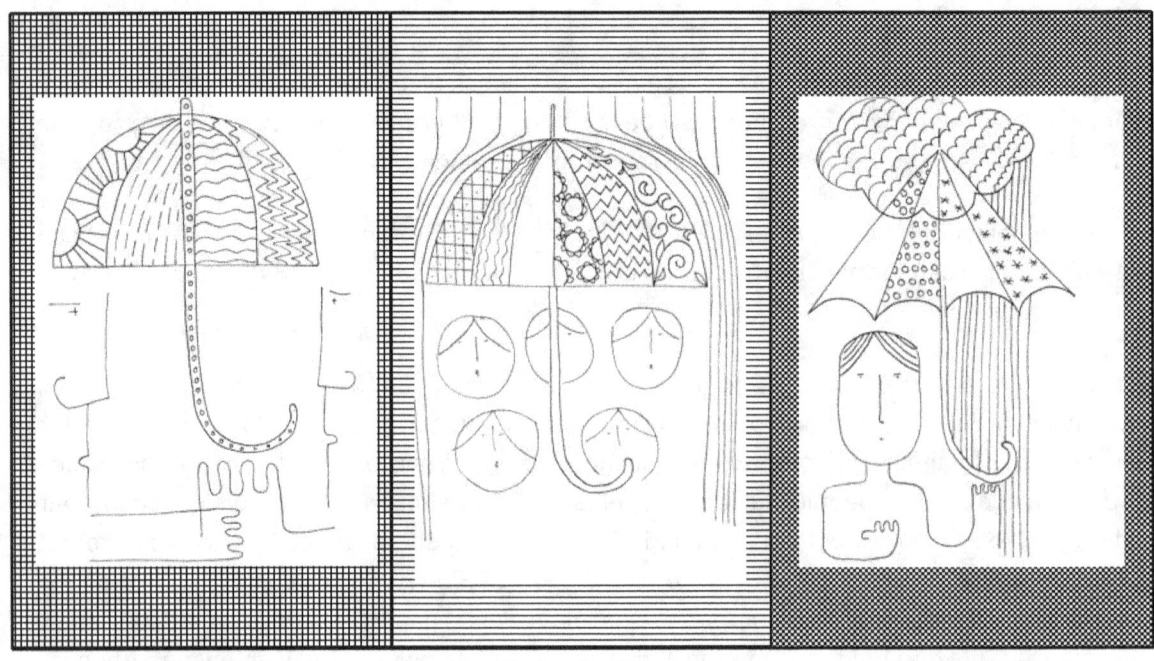

Umbrella 1   Umbrella 2   Umbrella 3

How to Draw Umbrella 1

Before you start to draw NeoWhimsy Umbrella 1, learn how to draw the repetitive patterns, which artist used in this drawing. You will find them below.

Umbrella 1	Suns	Waves
Symbolic hands	Rain	Zig-Zags
Circles	Profiles	

Next pages will teach you how to draw NeoWhimsy Umbrella 1. You will learn how to draw the contour of the umbrella, how to divide it into sections, and then how to fill those sections with the different repetitive patterns, making your umbrella look whimsical and artistic. When you create your NeoWhimsies you develop your imagination, artistic skills and artistic intuition. Intuition indicates knowledge that comes quickly into your mind without the intervention of conscious deliberation.

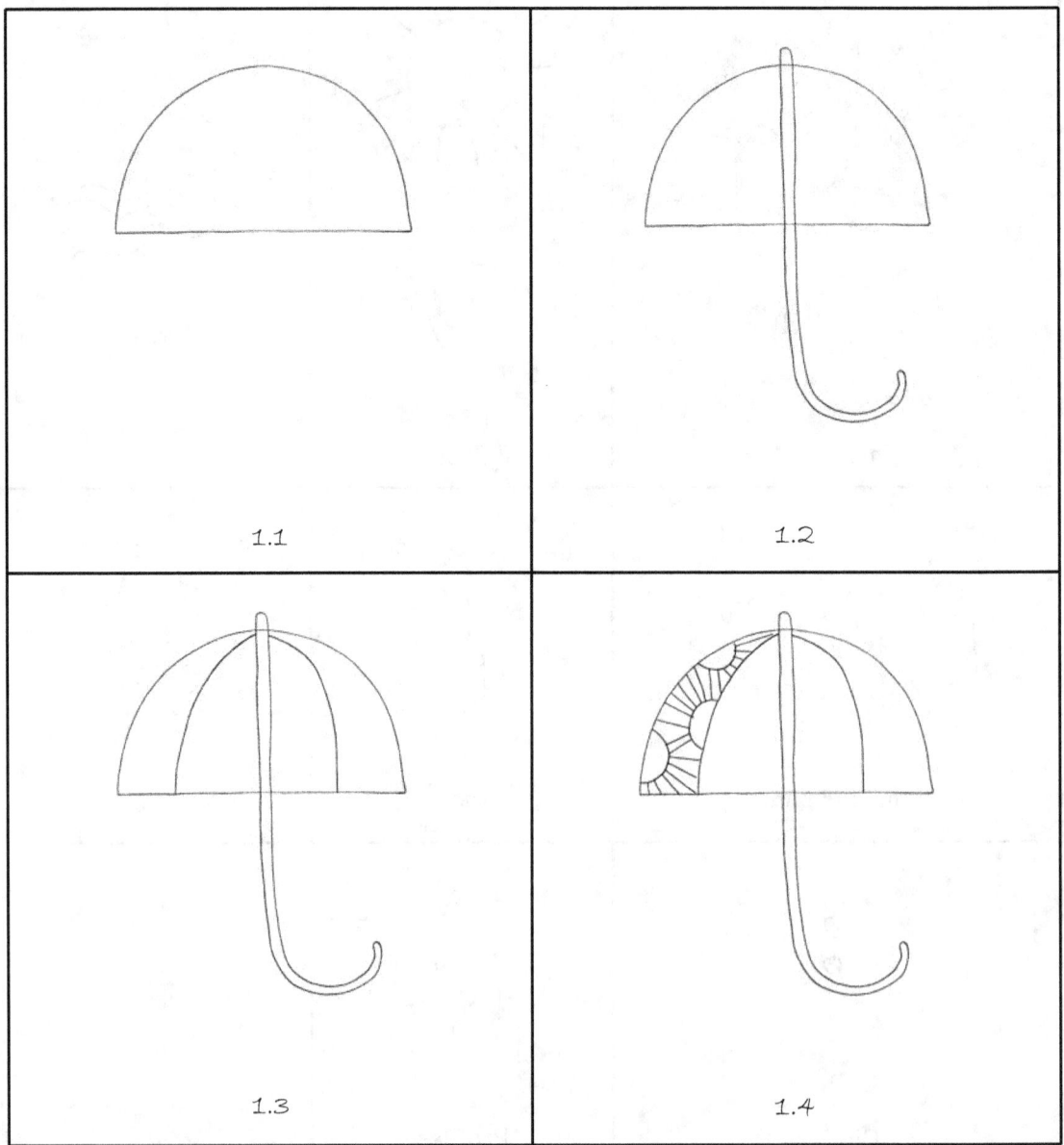

1.1

1.2

1.3

1.4

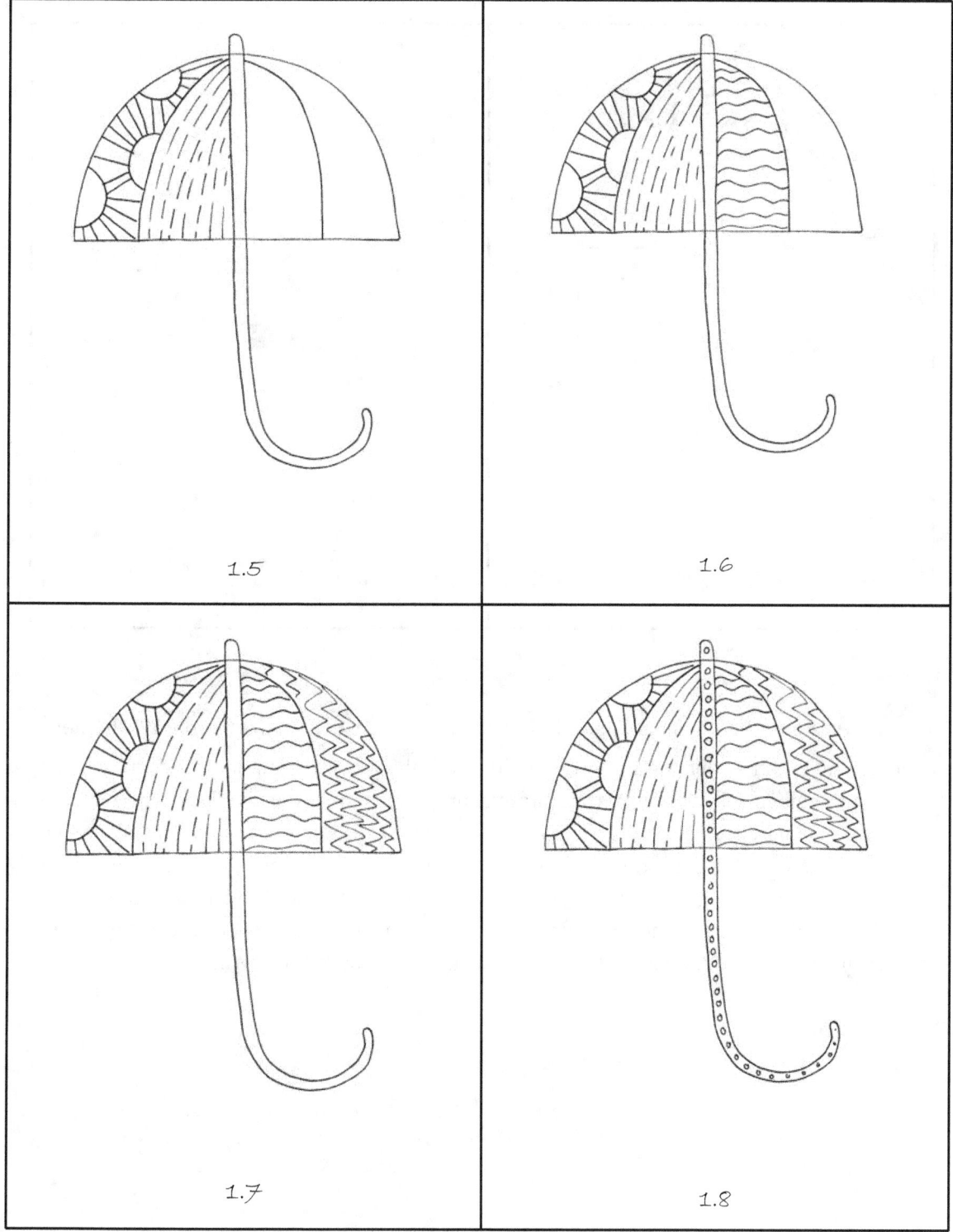

1.5

1.6

1.7

1.8

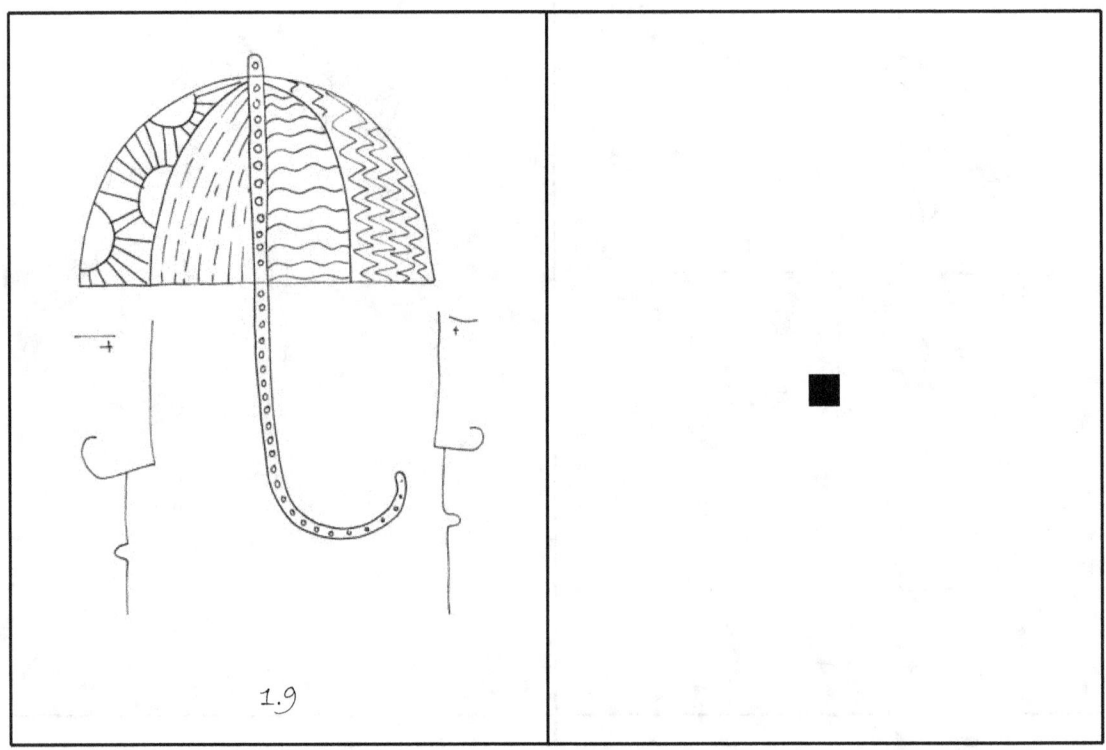

1.9

Your brain is the physical base of your mind. If you were to stretch out all the nerve connections in your brain, it would be about 3.2 million kilometers. The NeoPopRealism ink drawing is meditative drawing; meditation is the brain-changing activity, it increases learning functions. When you draw NeoPopRealism ink images you use the subliminal thinking, which is different than if you were using the conscious mind. The conscious mind is like part of the iceberg that is above the surface of the ocean. When you draw NeoPopRealism ink images, you use the part of your mind, which is hidden as the under-surface part of the iceberg.

NeoWhimsies for Beginners: 10 NeoPopRealism Ink Drawing Projects

How to Draw Umbrella 2

Next pages will teach you how to draw NeoWhimsy Umbrella 2. Follow the visual instructions and you will learn how to create the exuberant artworks. Serge created the following NeoWhimsy Umbrella 2 using Ink pen. When he created this drawing, he used his imagination. When you create NeoPopRealism Ink drawing do not worry if you make a "mistake". You do not have to erase it. It visually "disappears" when you continue drawing the repetitive patterns because these patterns balance the entire composition of the drawing. The composition and balance are very important and can be achieved through the training.

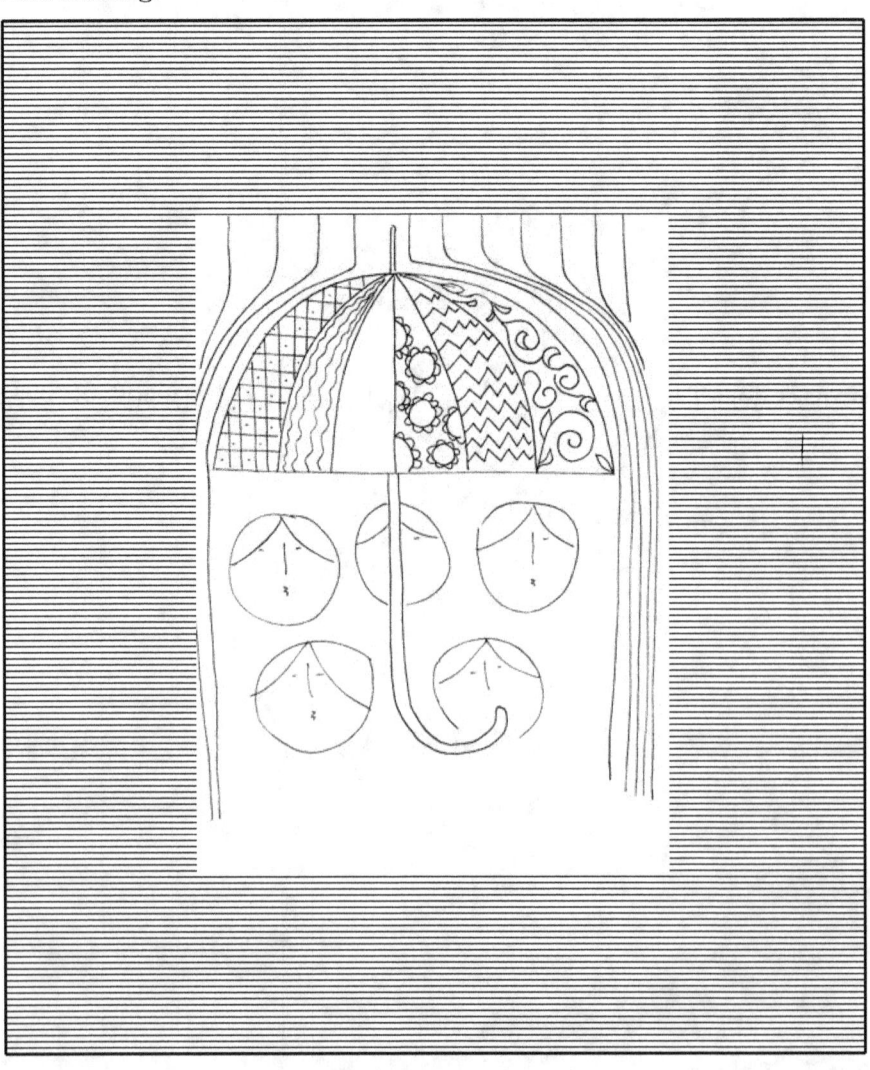

Serge E. Mikhailov, *Umbrella 2*, ink on paper

This page includes the repetitive patterns, used in NeoWhimsy Umbrella 2.

Squares with dots	Waves	Zig-Zags
Leaves	Flowers	Faces
Whirles		

Follow the visual Instructions and you will be able to learn how to create a beautiful image of the umbrella.

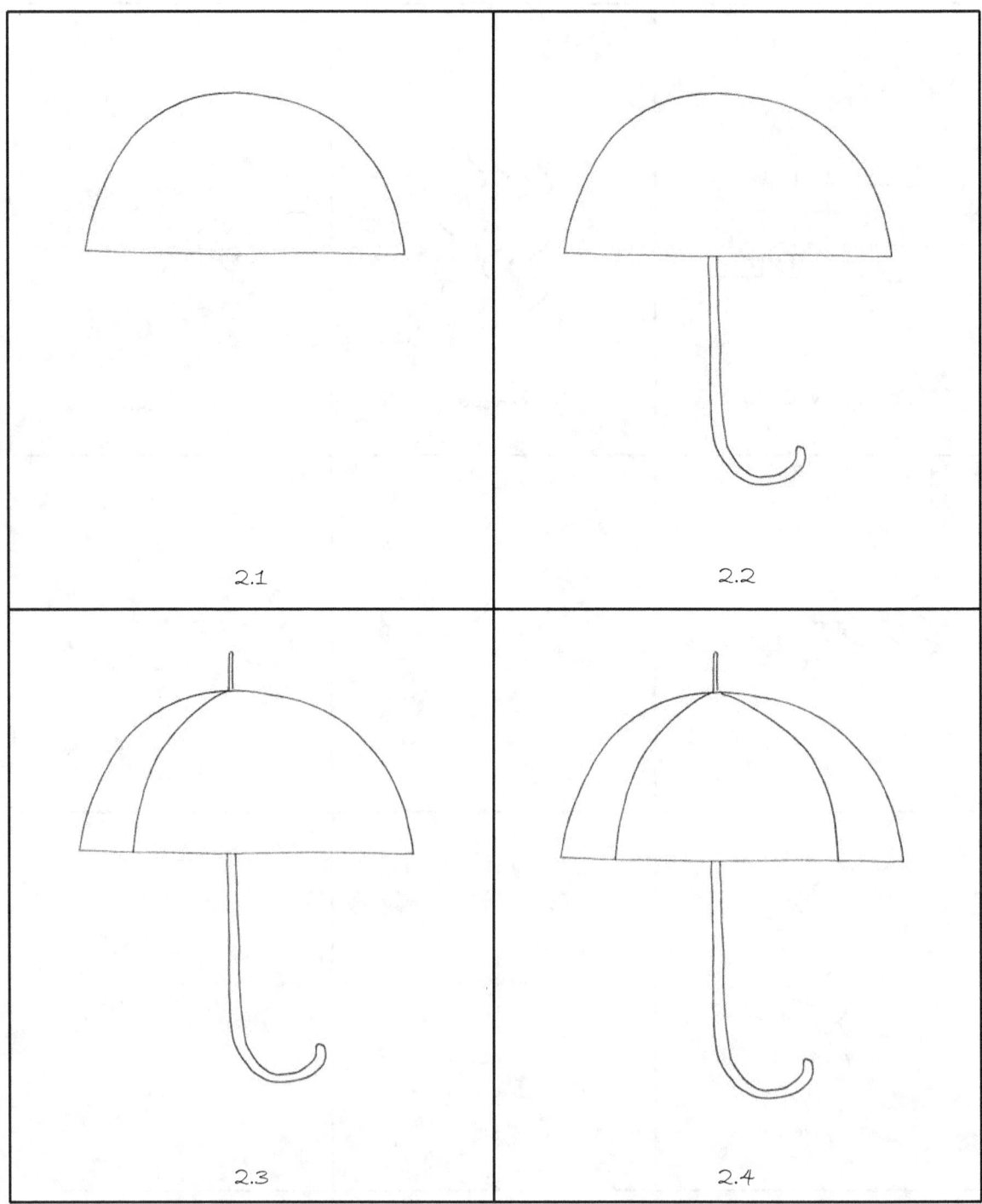

2.1

2.2

2.3

2.4

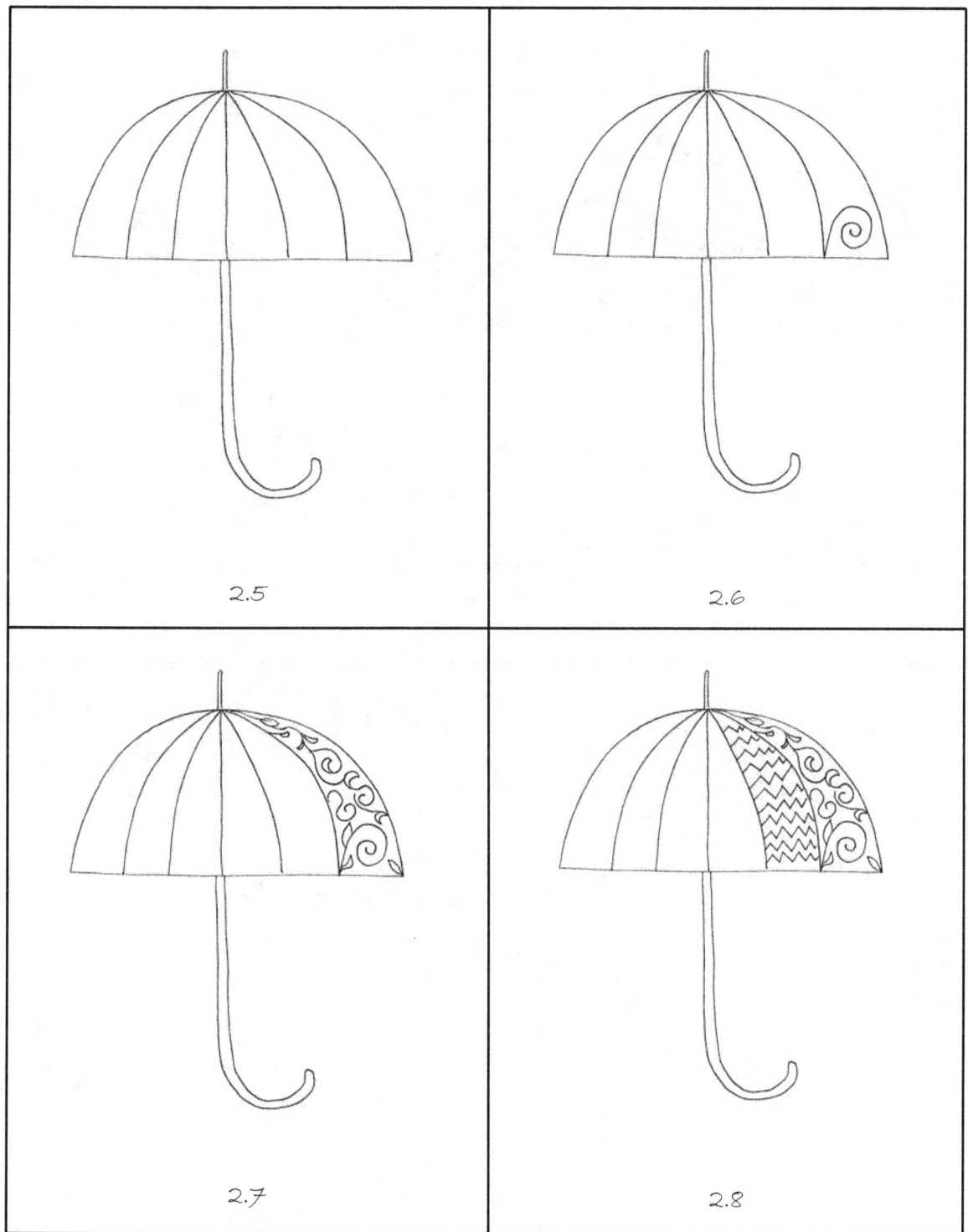

2.5

2.6

2.7

2.8

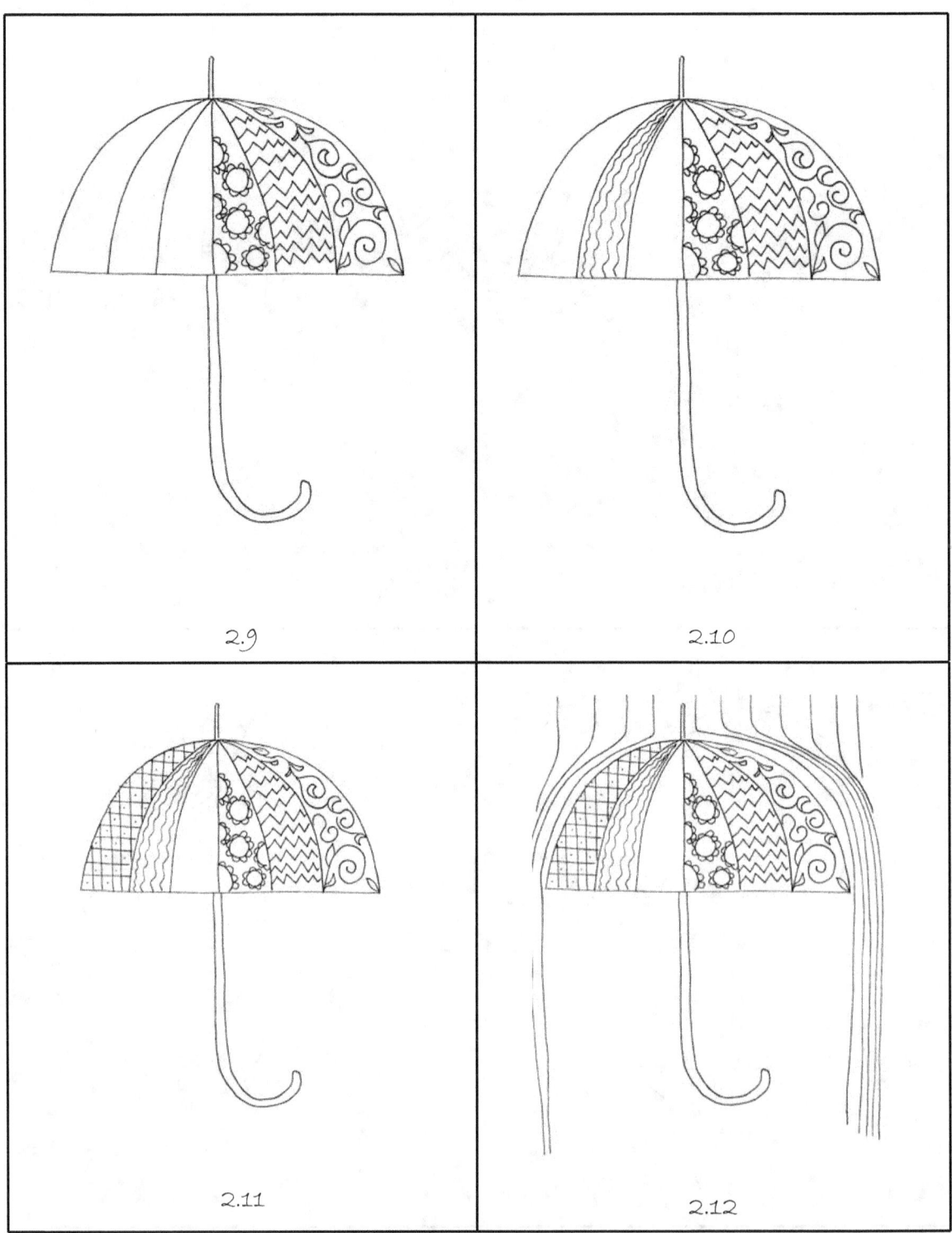

2.9

2.10

2.11

2.12

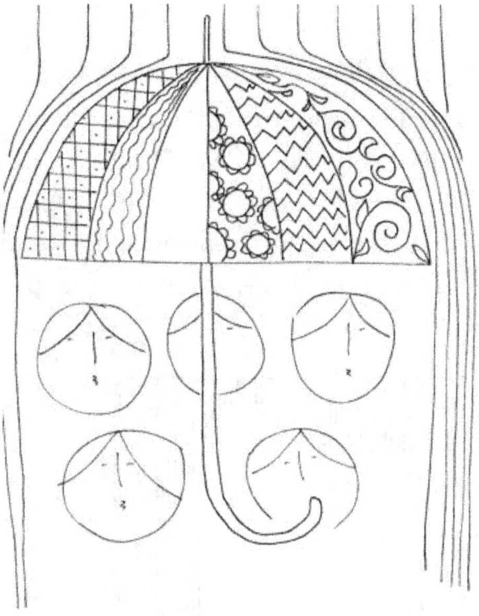

2.13

NeoPopRealism ink drawing is a new visual language. Language is the principal means of personal communication. Artistic language reflects a unique culture, it is a key to an experience the world, it is about how people think about life and how they experience it.

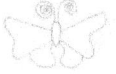

How to Draw *Umbrella 3*

Next few pages will show you how to draw NeoWhimsy Umbrella 3. Serge E. Mikhailov created the this NeoWhimsy using the line and repetitive patterns. When he created this drawing, he used his imagination. When you create NeoPopRealism ink drawings do not worry if you make a "mistake". You do not have to erase it. It visually "disappears" with new repetitive patterns because these patterns balance the entire composition of the drawing. The balancing composition in art is very important and can be achieved through the training.

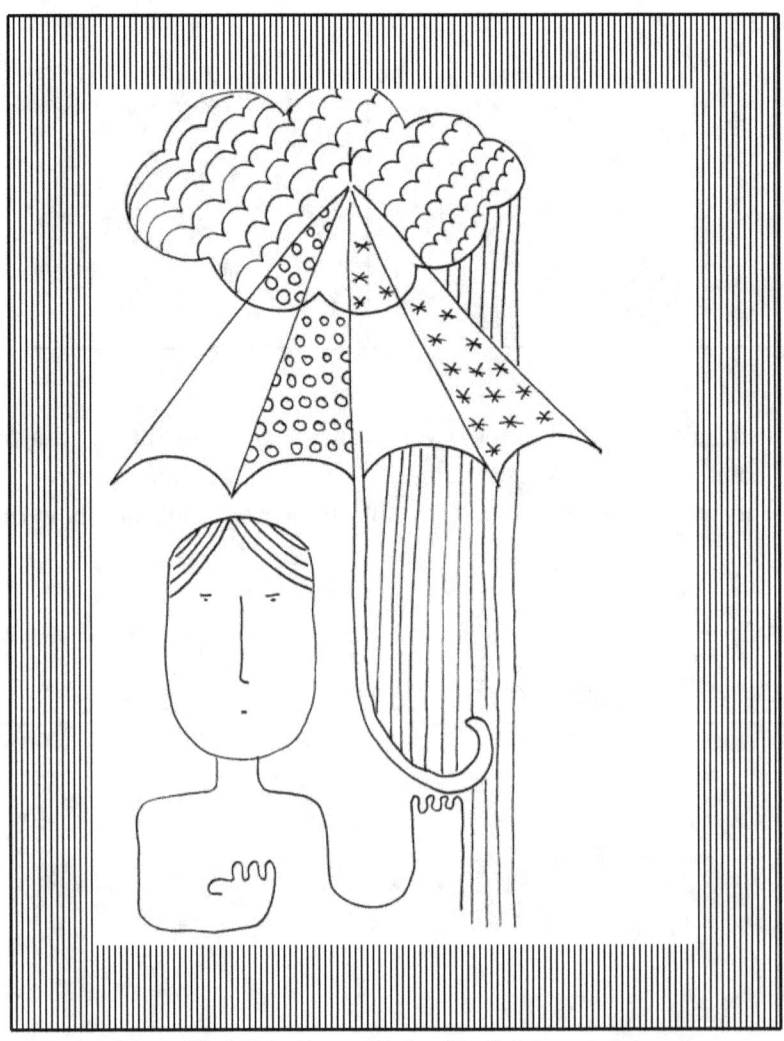

Serge E. Mikhailov, *Umbrella 3*, ink on paper

Learn how to draw the repetitive patterns used in this drawing. You will find them below.

Breeze up-side-down	Circles	Stars
Symbolic hands 1	Symbolic hands 2	Girl's face
Strips		

The following pages contain the visual instructions. They will help you to learn how to create a beautiful artwork with umbrella.

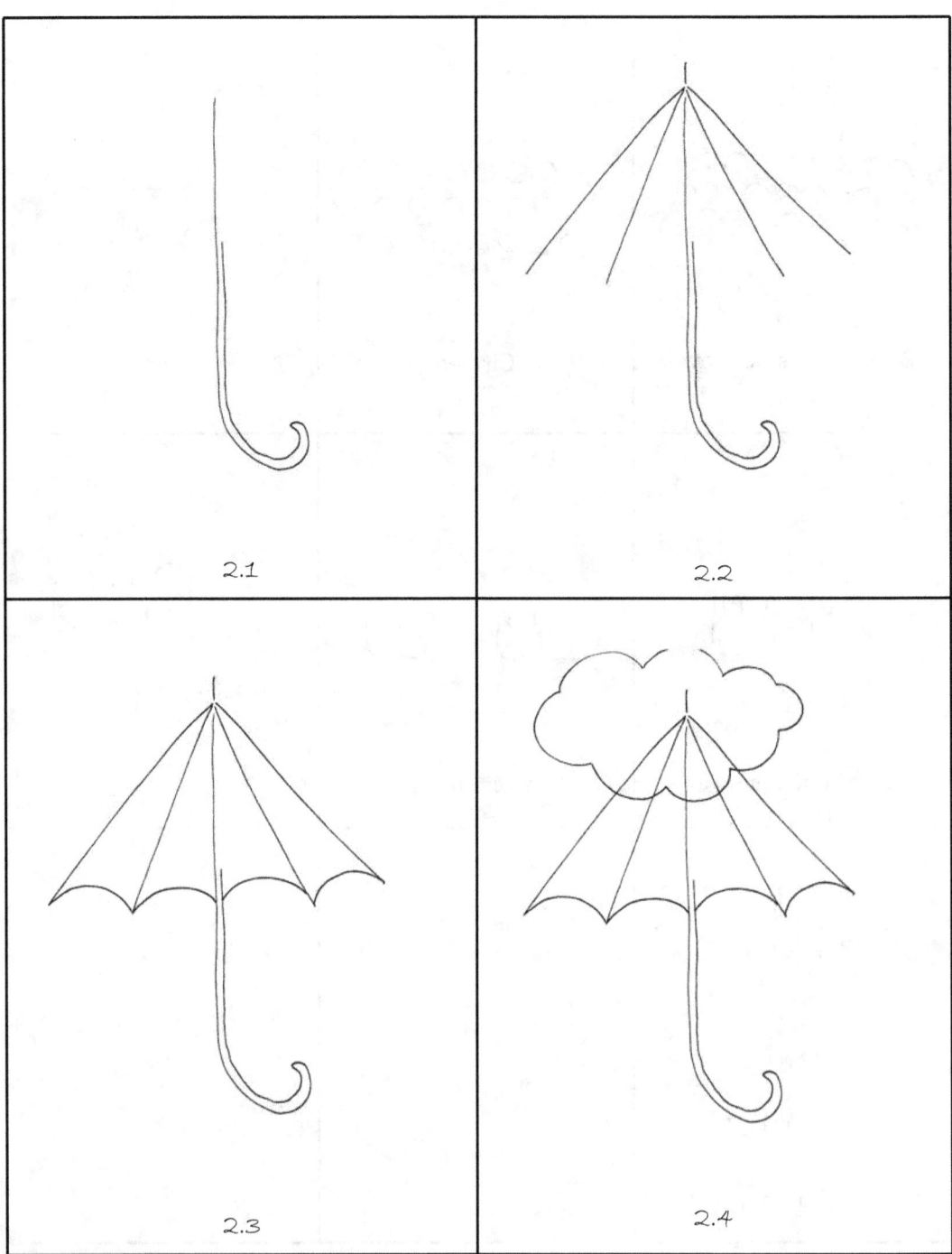

2.1

2.2

2.3

2.4

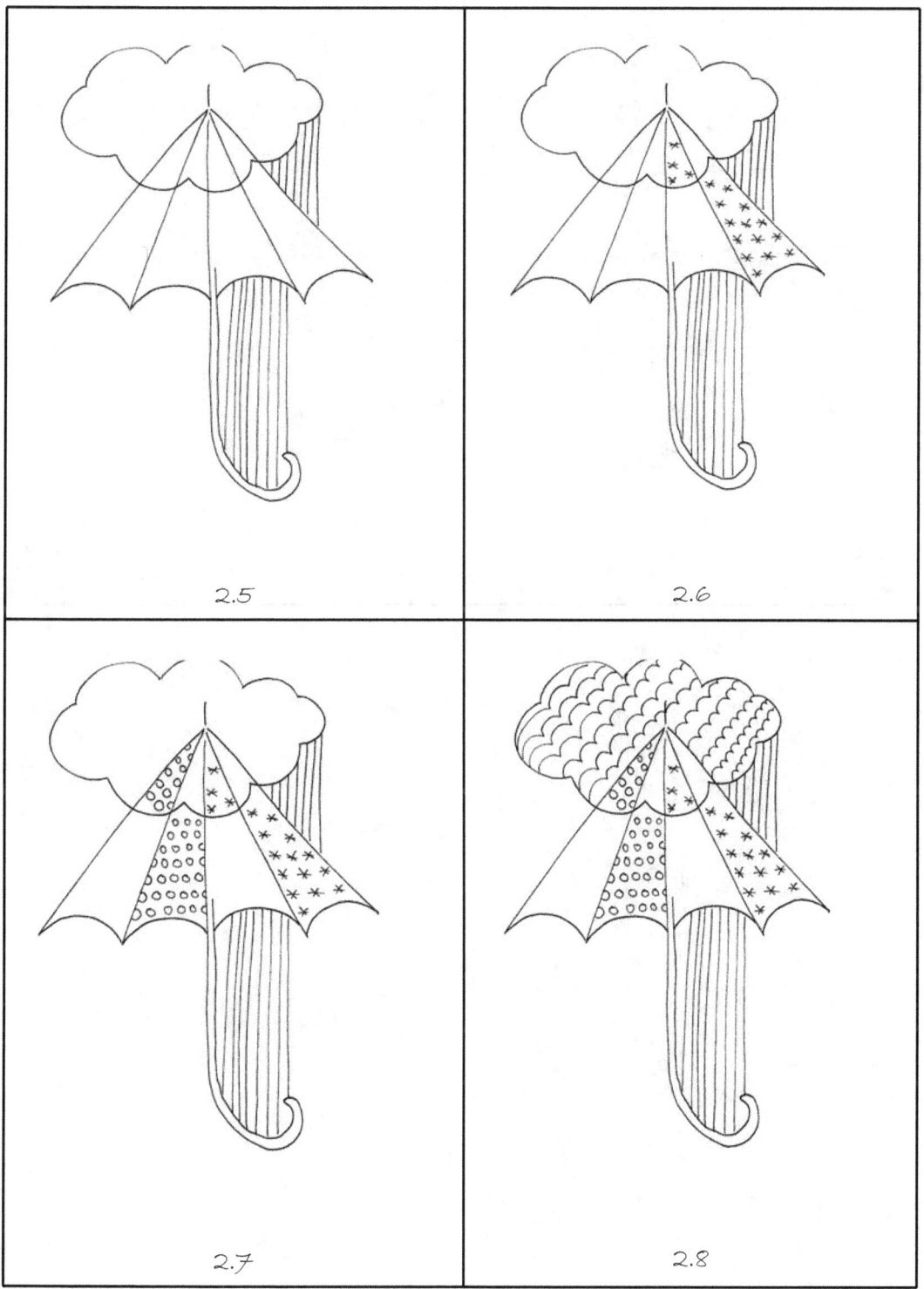

2.5

2.6

2.7

2.8

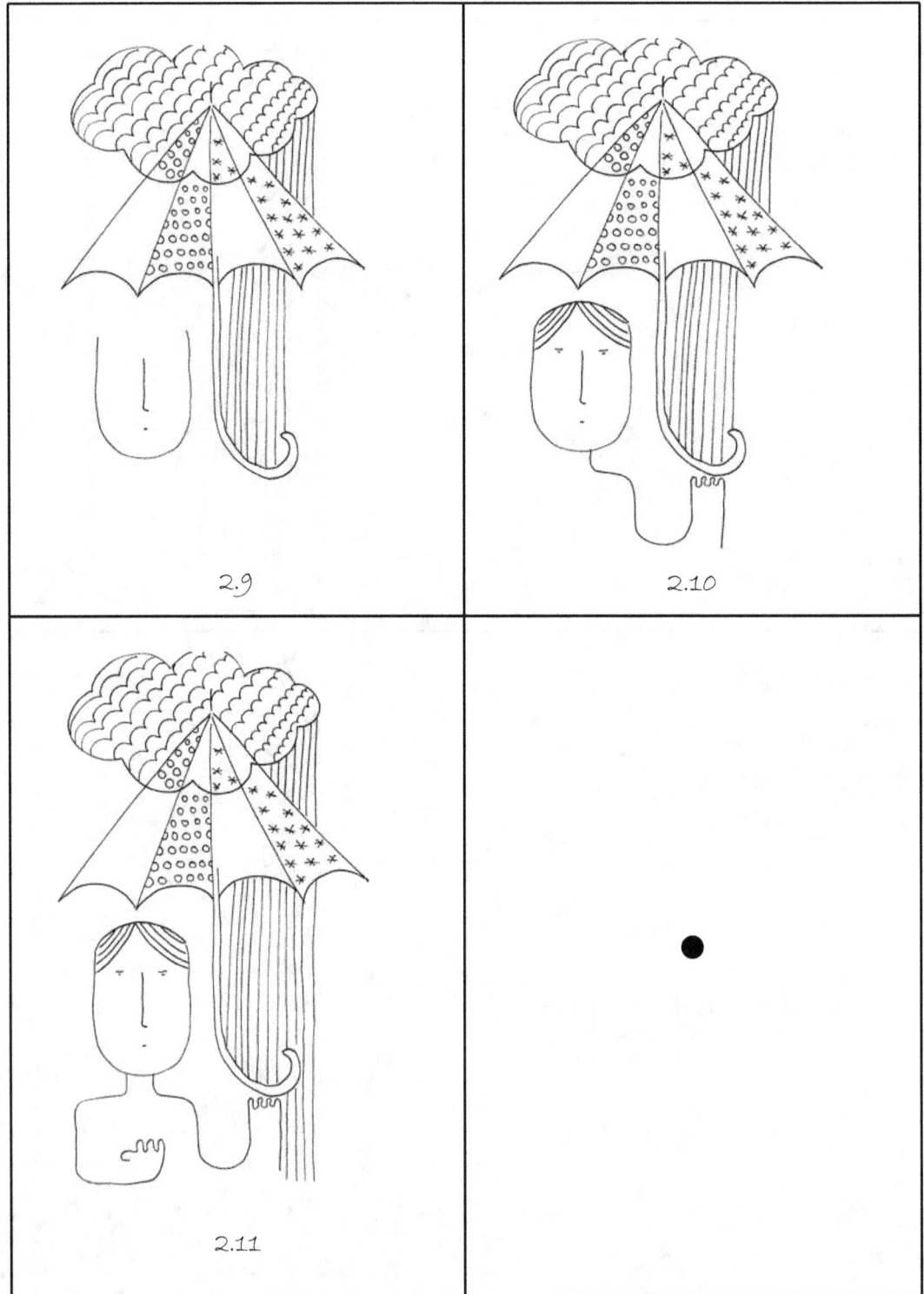

2.9

2.10

2.11

Draw the Umbrellas Here and Now

Use next pages for your training. Get your ink pen and fill sections of the drawings with different imaginative repetitive patterns. When you create the patterns, rely on to your creative instinct (use different ornaments based on combinations of circles, triangles, rectangular, squares, dots, different small objects, more) or use patterns you already know. However, to succeed in art, you must always create something new. Some section(s) leave blank. The repetitive patterns' (ornaments) drawing is meditative process, when you draw, you enter the meditative state of mind. There is a strong connection between meditation, health, and happiness; the drawing helps you increase your energy and learning abilities. When you learn and develop more expertise, your brain builds large and robust information and skill bank in your memory. Then, your unconscious thought process will be able to examine options based on your past experiences. More you practice, better your artworks are. Imagination is a very important artistic quality; it is considered a creative faculty of the mind. It is a process of the mind used for thinking and creating. More you practice, better your imagination is.

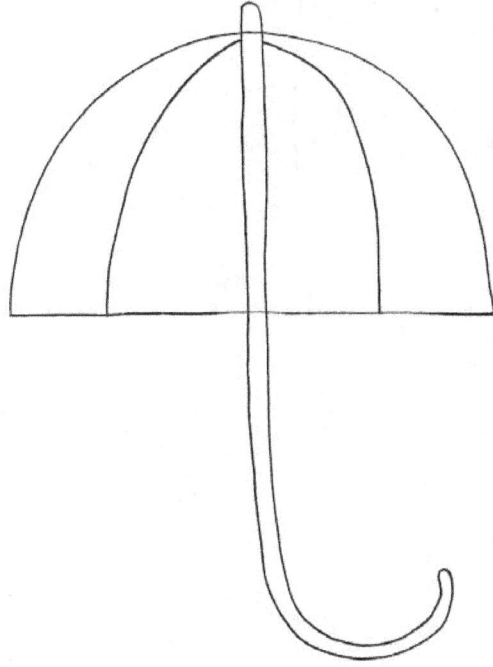

The Umbrella A

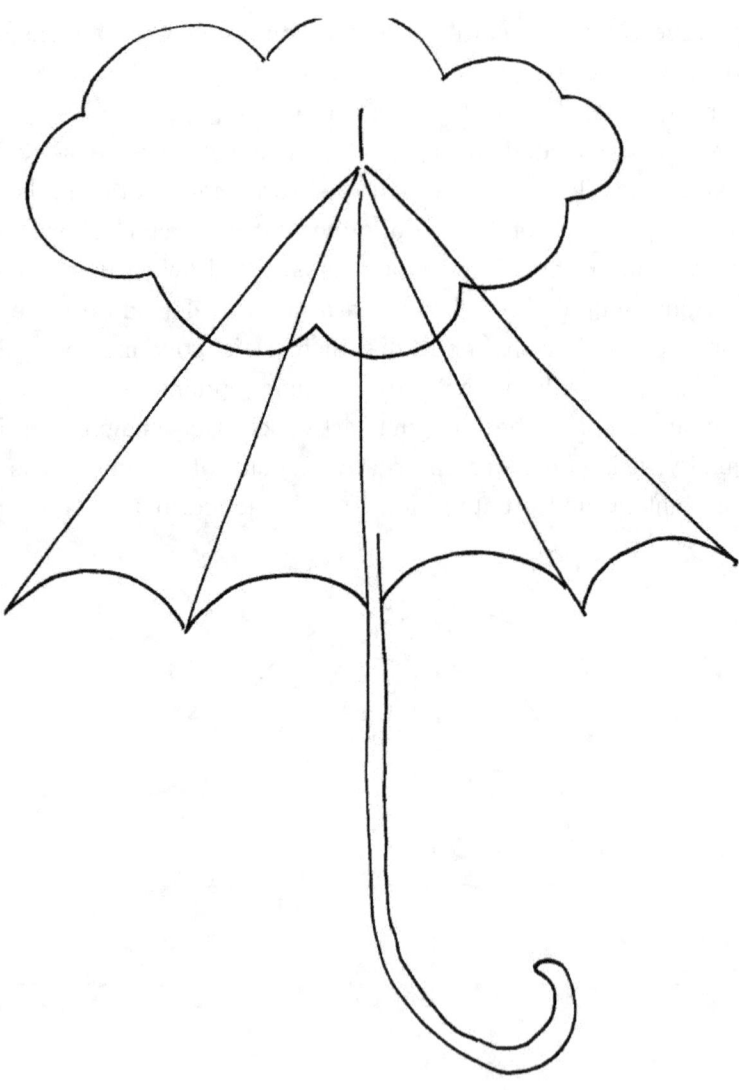

The Umbrella B

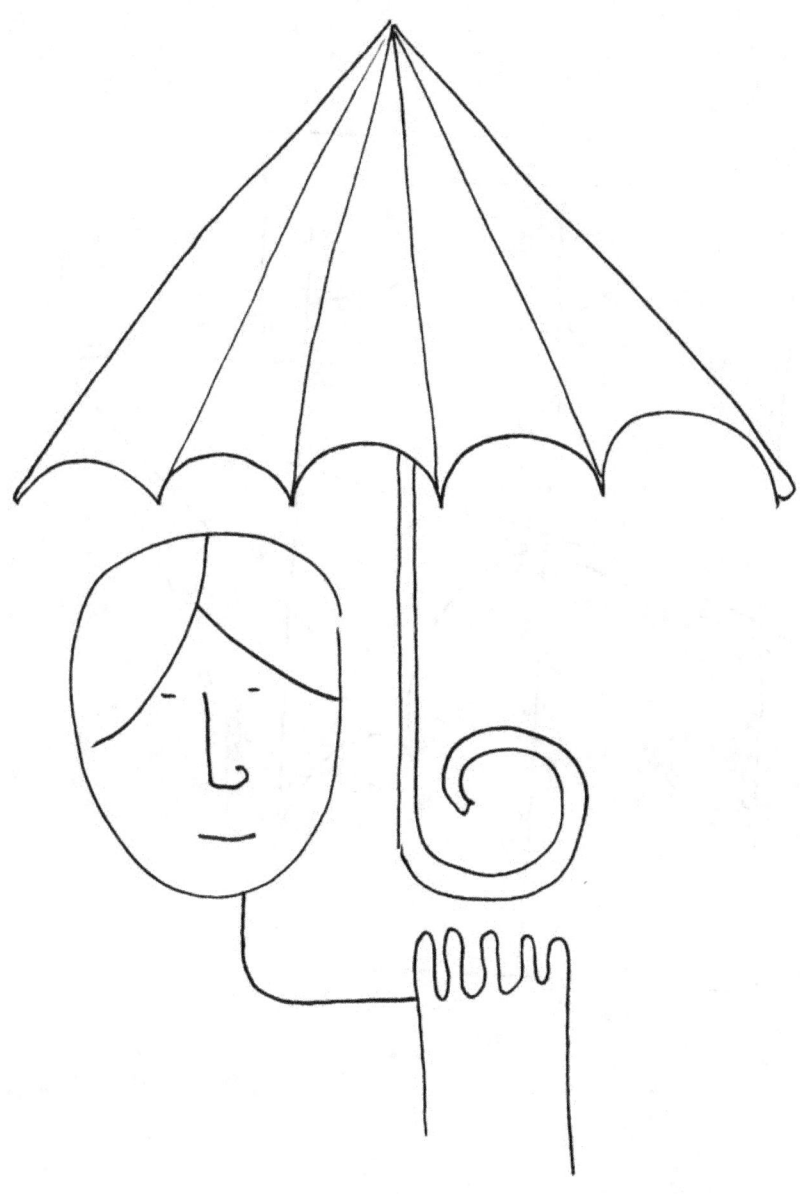

The Umbrella C

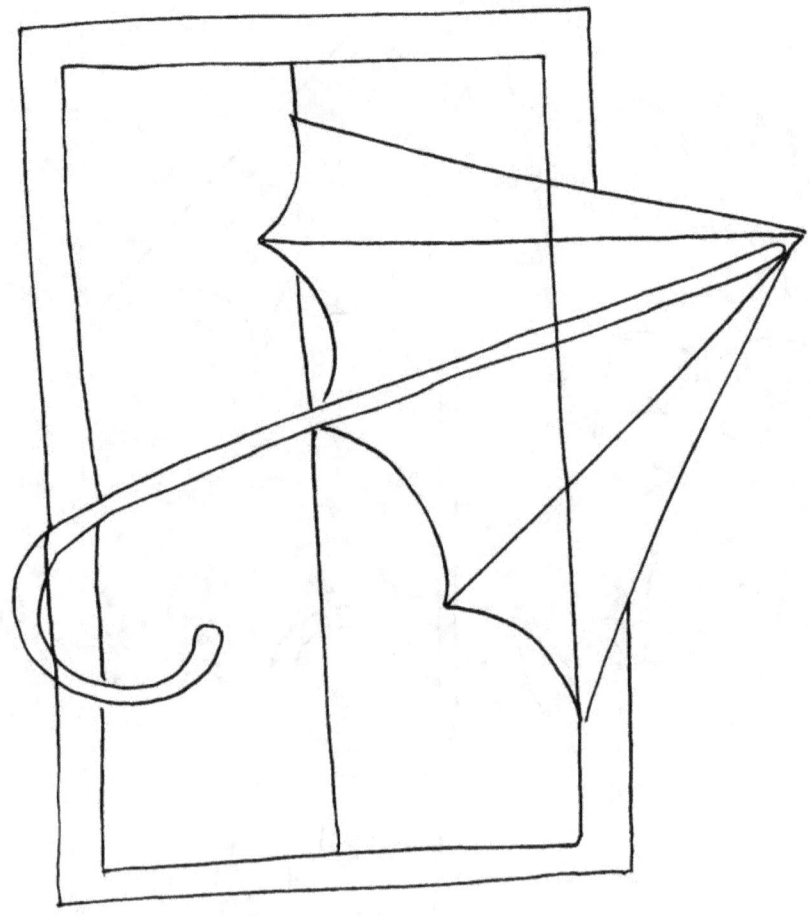

The Umbrella D

Draw the Butterflies

$\mathcal{B}$utterflies are found on all continents except Antarctica, and scientists estimate that there are approximately 12–15,000 species of butterflies. There are still thousands of butterfly species that have not been found or described. When artist created the following NeoWhimsies Butterflies, he used his imagination. He drew a line that created the sections and then he filled these sections with different repetitive patterns. Each butterfly has different character and look. The following pages with visual instructions will guide you through the entire drawing process from the beginning to end. Every next image includes new detail(s). The final images look like this:

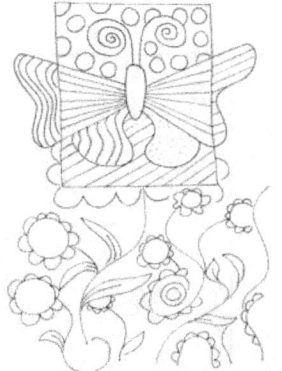

The Butterfly 1

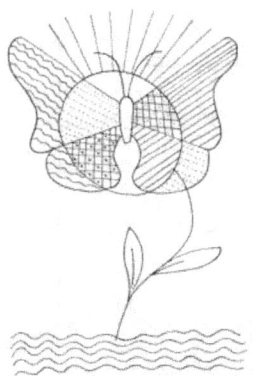

The Butterfly 2

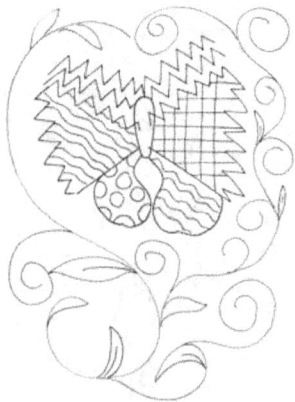

The Butterfly 3

How to Draw Butterfly 1

This page includes the repetitive patterns used in NeoWhimsy Butterfly 1

Circles	Parallel strips	Dots
Left wing's strips	Right wing's strips	Edge ornament
Flowers	Waves	Whirles and leaves

These pages show step by step how to create a NeoWhimsy Butterfly 1. Follow the visual instructions and when you'll understand the process of the image development, you will be able to draw the images on your own. All you will need for it is a piece of paper, ink pen, artistic skill and imagination. Free your mind, get creative!

1.1

1.2

1.3

1.4

1.5

1.6

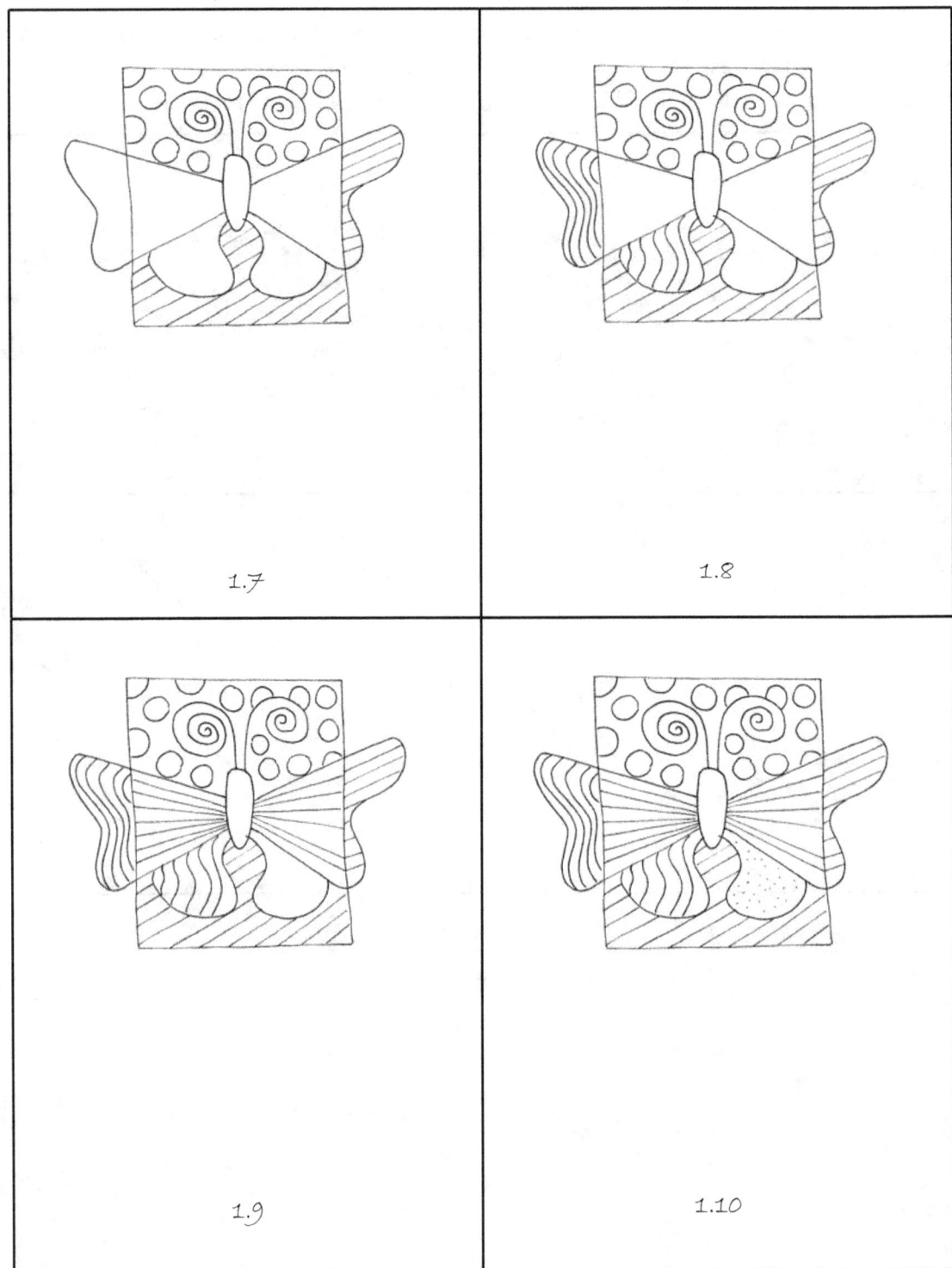

1.7

1.8

1.9

1.10

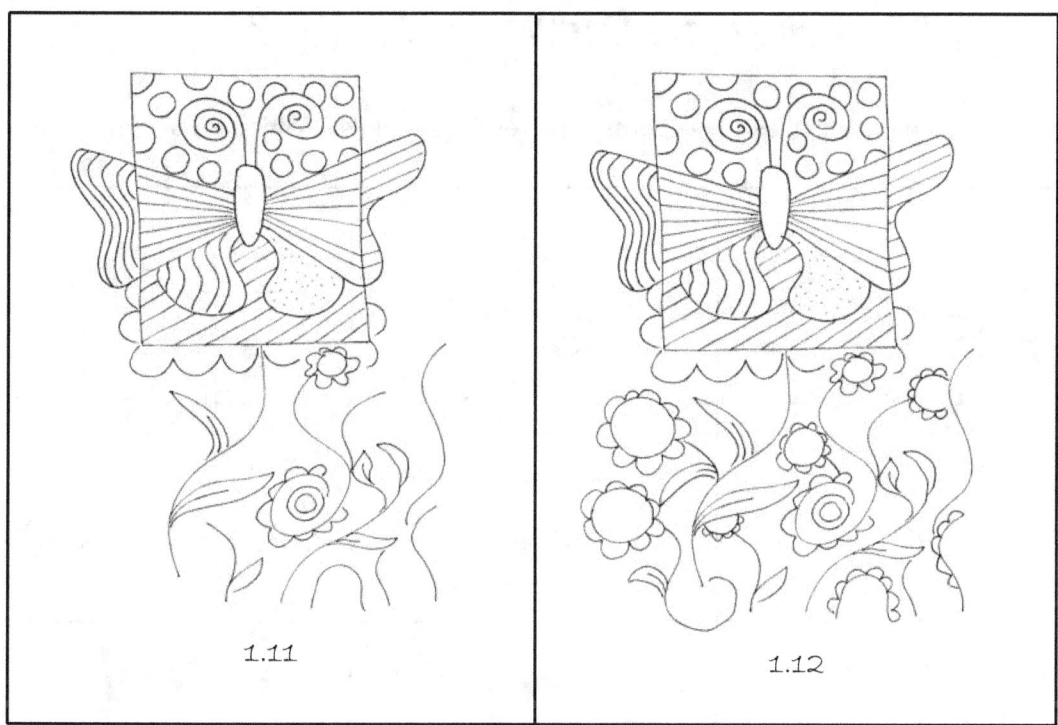

1.11   1.12

How to Draw Butterfly 2

This page includes the repetitive patterns used in NeoWhimsy Butterfly 2.

Waves	Dots	Squares and crosses
Squares and dots	Leaves	Sun
Strips		

Next pages will show how Serge E. Mikhailov created NeoWhimsy Butterfly 2. Follow the visual instructions. Your understanding of the process of image development will help you create NeoWhimsies on your own,

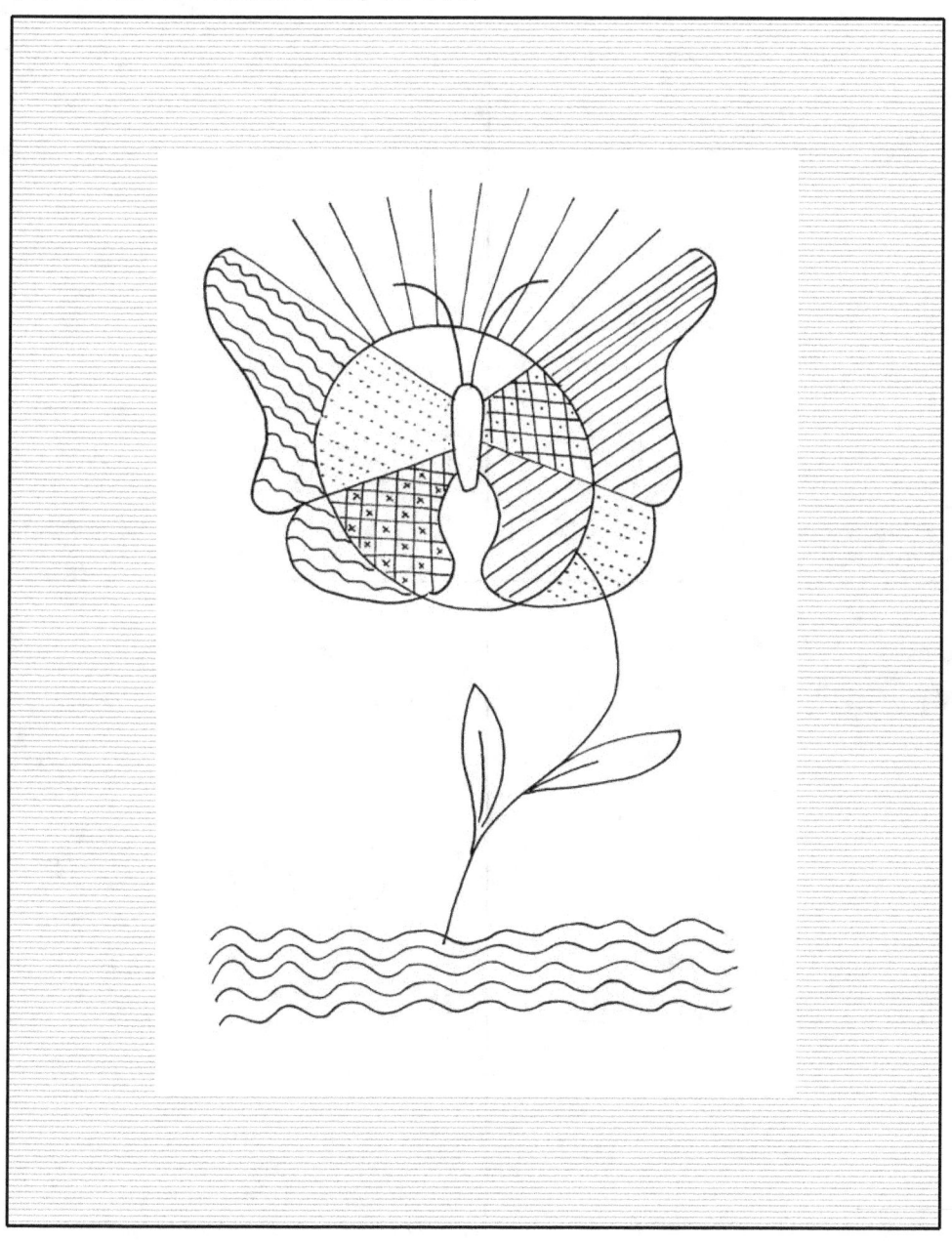

Serge E. Mikhailov, *The Butterfly 2*

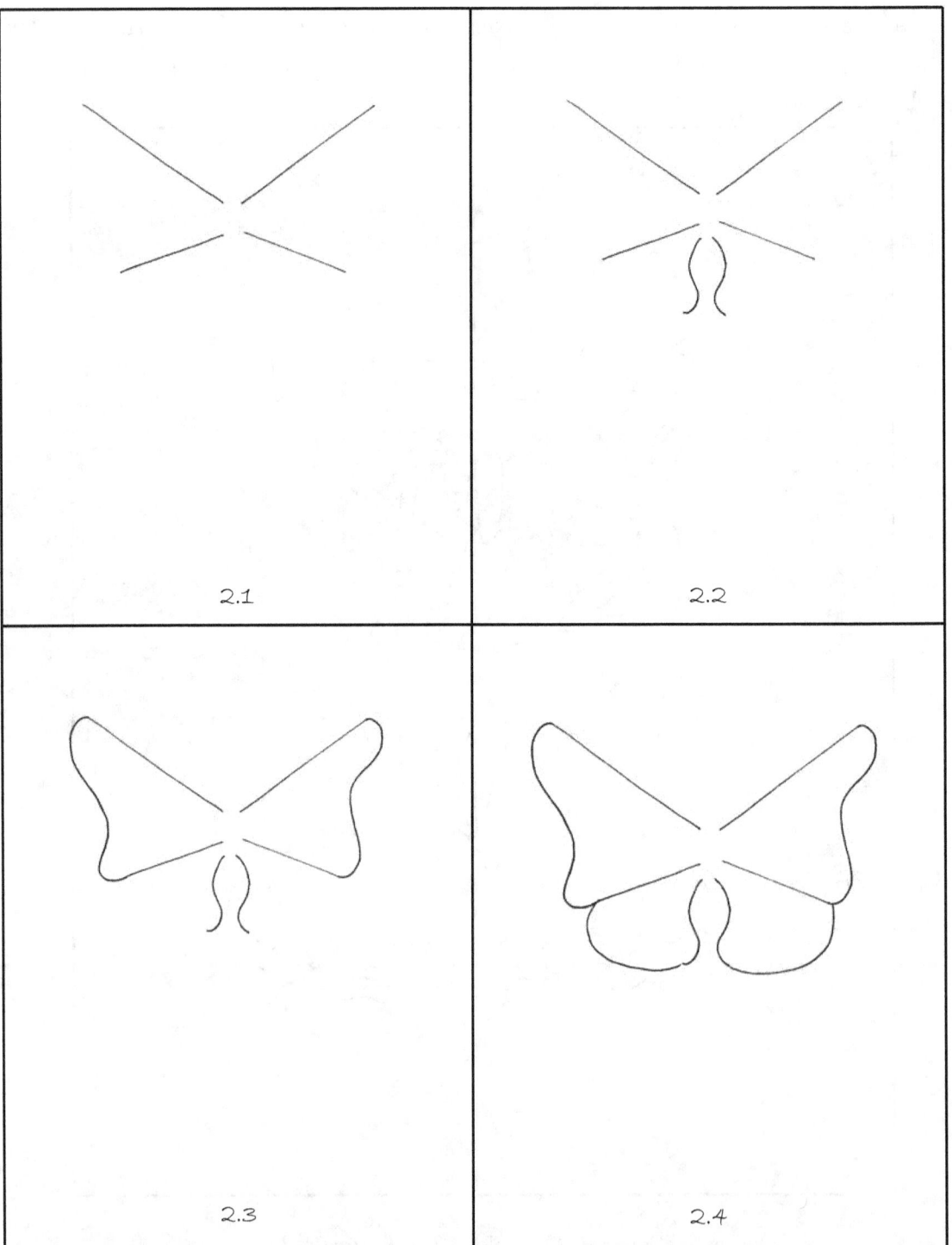

2.1

2.2

2.3

2.4

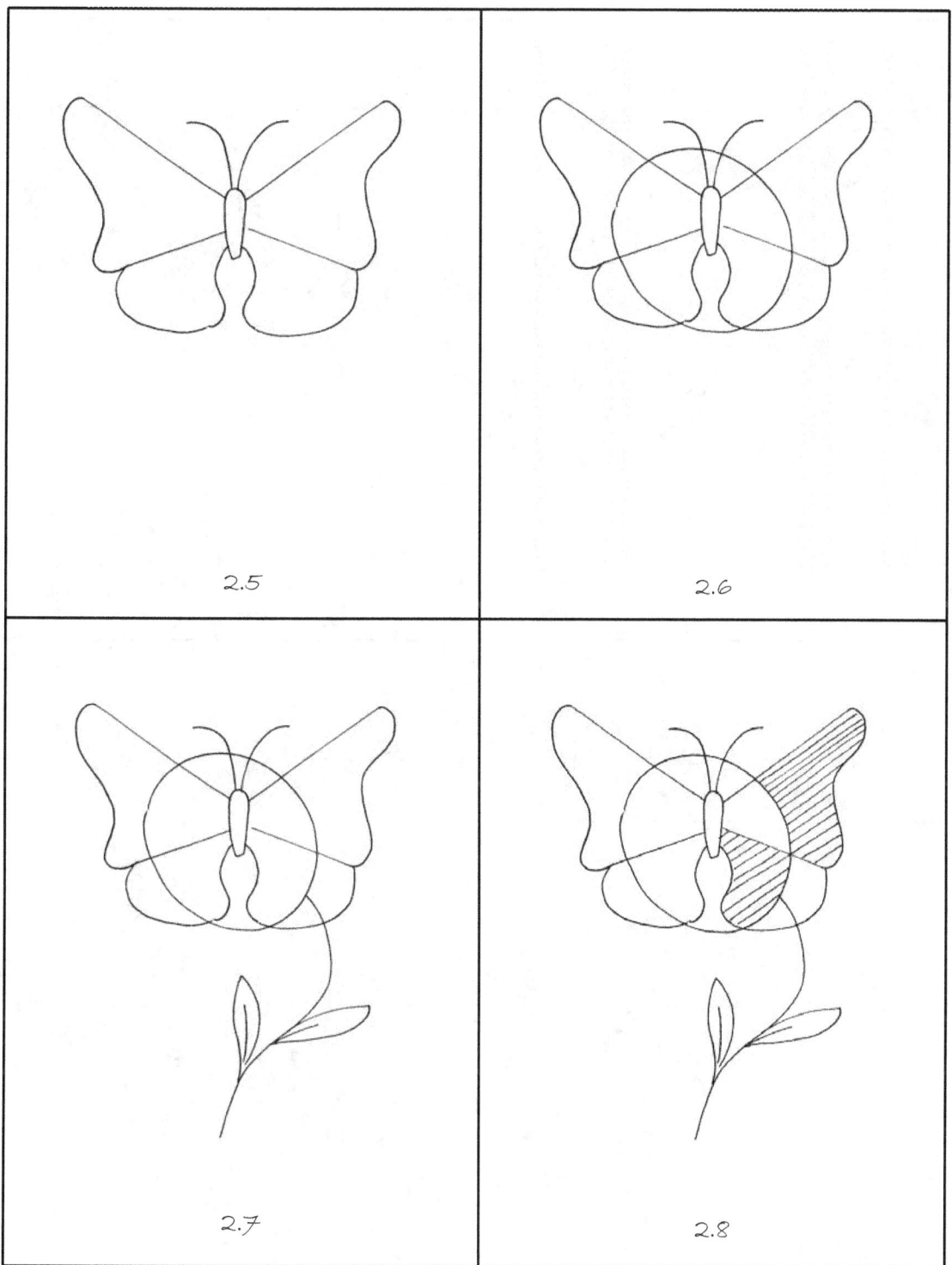

2.5

2.6

2.7

2.8

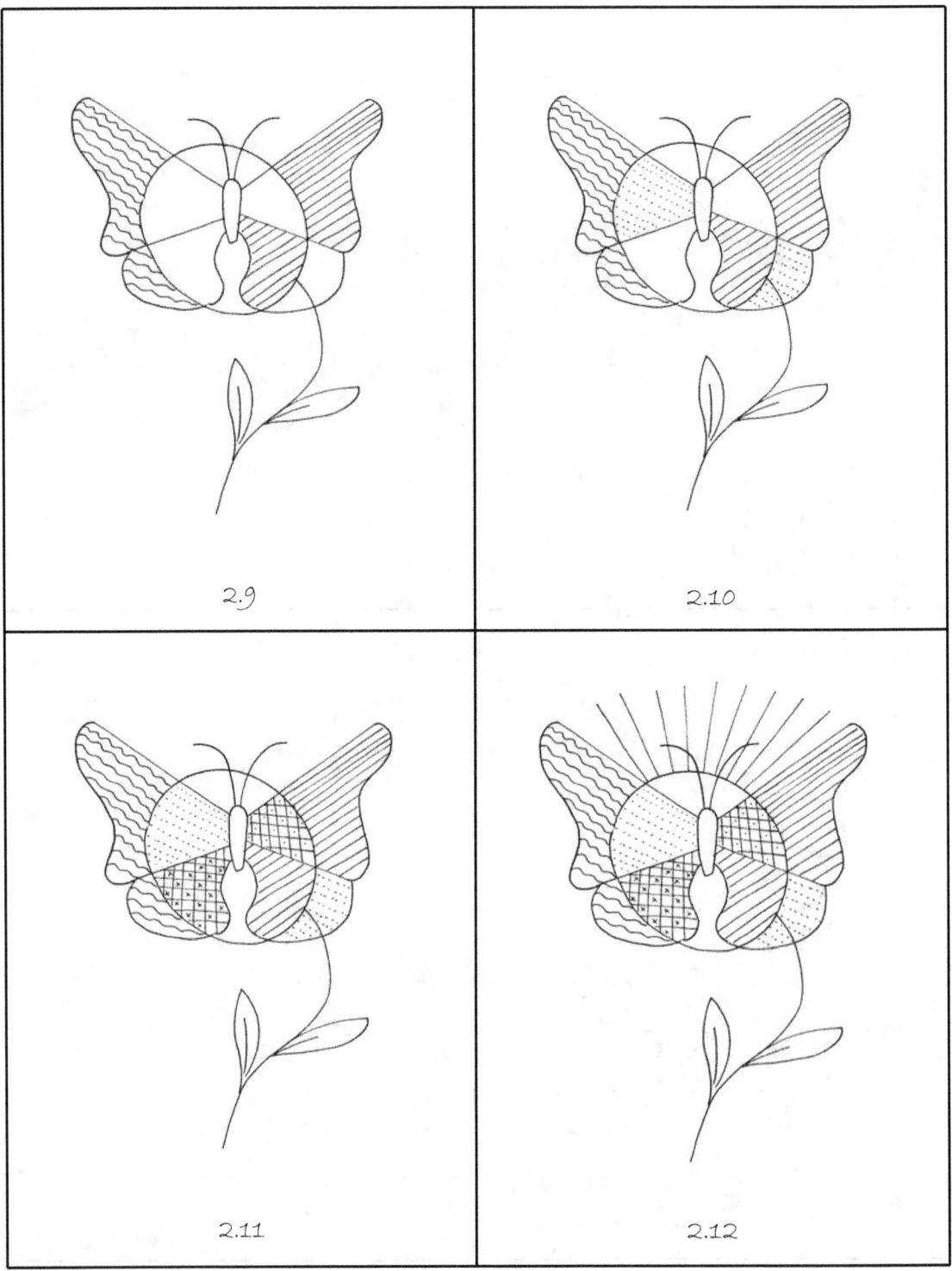

2.9

2.10

2.11

2.12

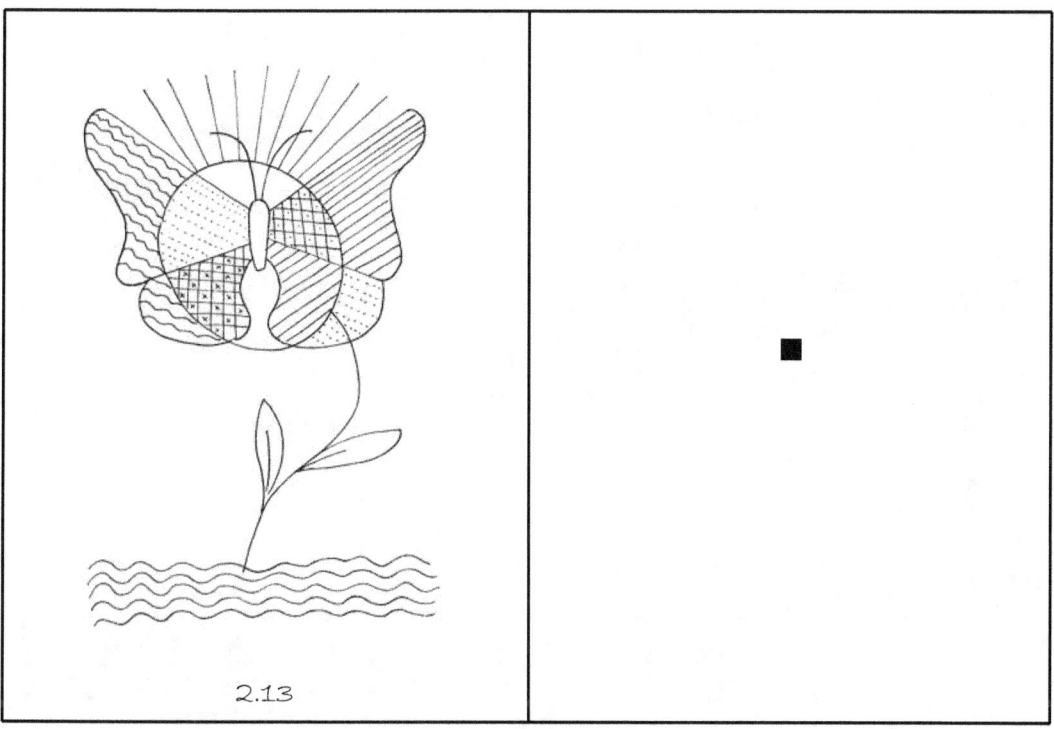

2.13

The drawing should be done in a quiet environment. However, using music would help. The drawing process brings you into a receptive meditative state of mind. Meditation helps to bring into balance our body, mind and spirit. It helps to express ourselves through the creativity.

People make the rules and break the rules.
But harmony is eternal. Nadia Russ

How to Draw Butterfly 3

The following pages will show you how to create NeoWhimsy Butterfly 3. The butterflies in this book are imaginative. They are all different and unique. Imagination is the ability of forming images and sensations when they are not perceived through sight, hearing, or other senses. Follow the visual instructions and learn how Serge creates his artwork: he draws a line that creates the sections. Then, he fills appeared sections with the patterns. This drawing is rhythmical like music and it has its accents like jazz has syncopation. Learn the process and soon you will be able to create NeoWhimsies independently, using your imagination and the recently developed artistic skills.

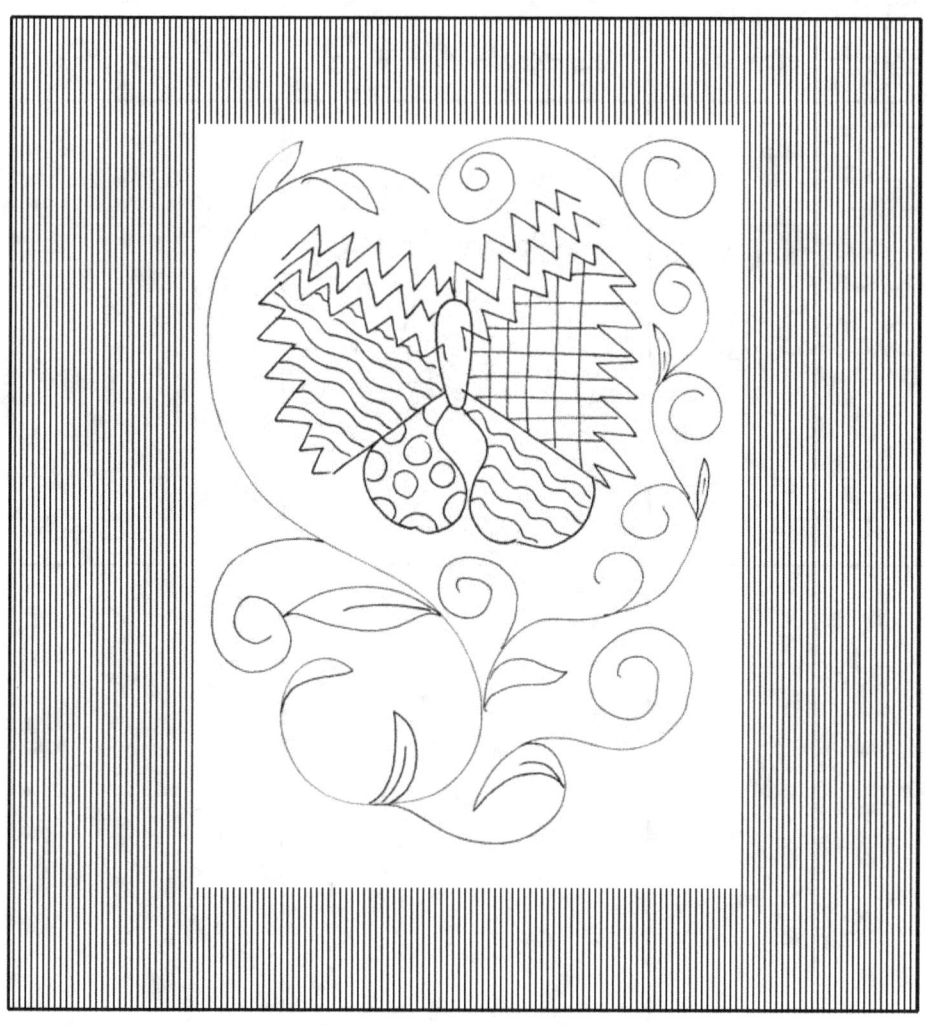

Serge E. Mikhailov, *The Butterfly 3*

This page includes the repetitive patterns, used in his NeoWhimsy Butterfly 3.

Zig-Zags – Left Wing	Zig-Zag – Right Wing	Squares
Circles	Waves	Leaves
Whirles		

Next pages include the visual instruction that will show you how to draw NeoWhimsy Butterfly 3. Art is a union between craft and imagination. When you practice, you develop your artistic skills and your imagination.

3.1

3.2

3.3

3.4

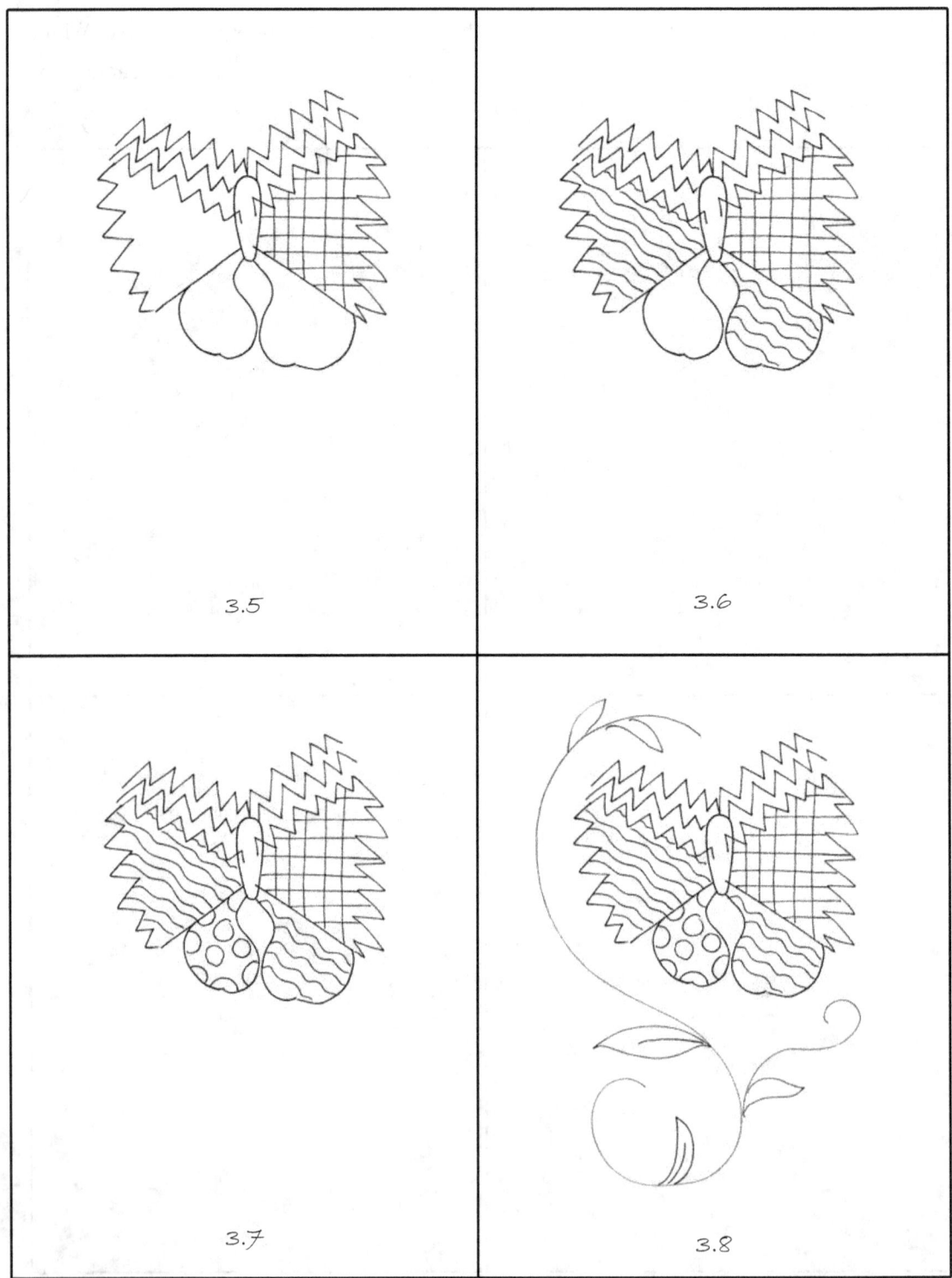

3.5

3.6

3.7

3.8

Draw the Butterflies Here and Now

The next pages your will use for your training – for your practicing. Fill sections of images of the butterflies with different repetitive patterns. Create new patterns using your (unlimited) imagination, create absolutely new image of a butterfly with asymmetrical ornaments on the wings. Also, if you have some (temporary) trouble with your imagination, then draw the patterns, used in this book. Turn on your artistic senses and follow your creative instinct. Some section(s) you can leave blank – it is the 'air'. Remember that nothing is impossible. When you draw the repetitive patterns your brain is relaxing, you enter the meditative state of mind. And at the end you will achieve both the good artistic results and the purity of your mind.

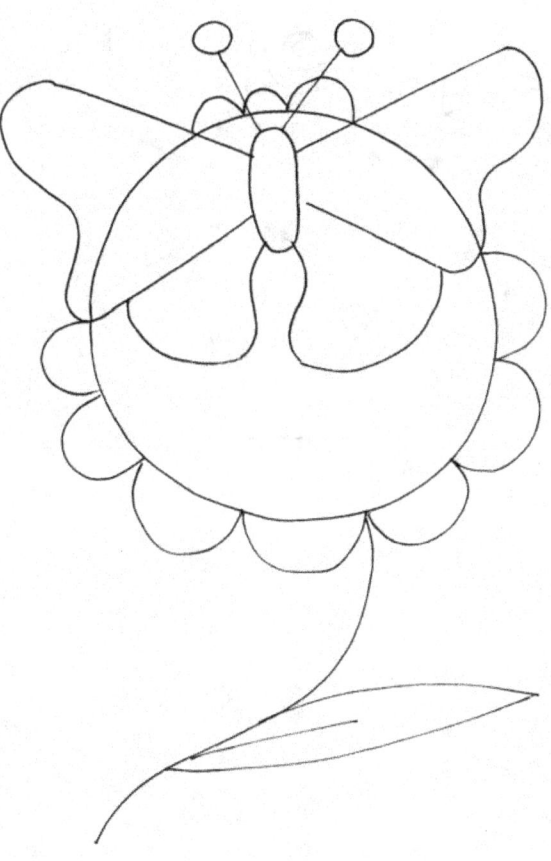

The Butterfly A

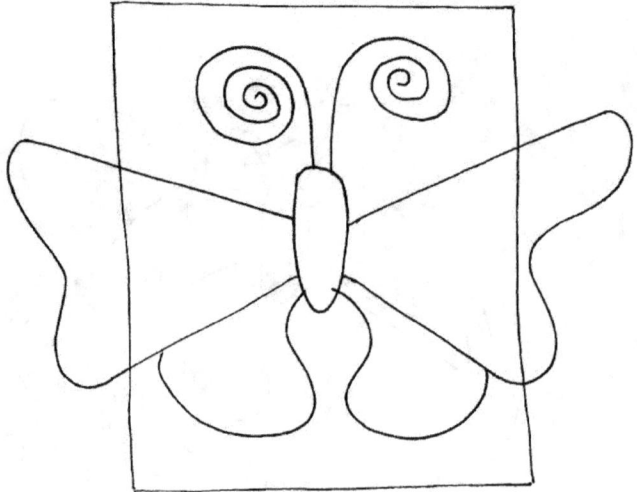

The Butterfly B

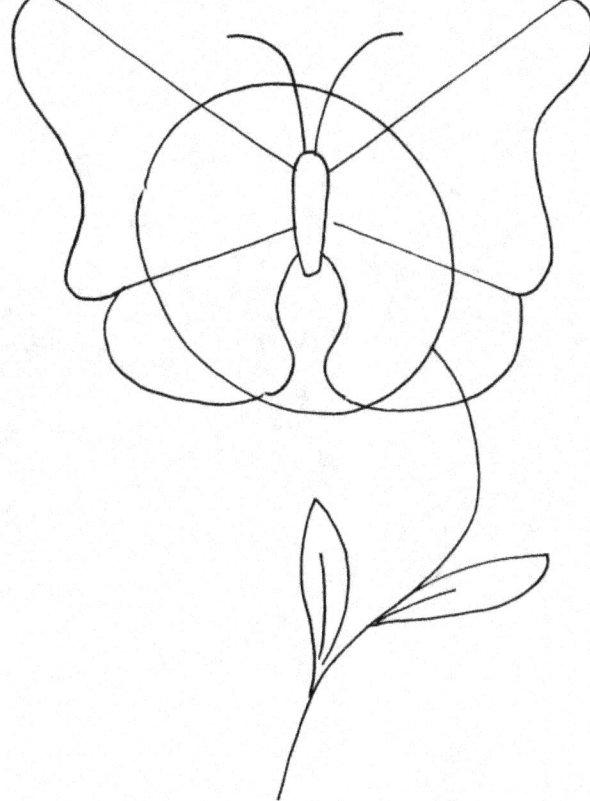

The Butterfly C

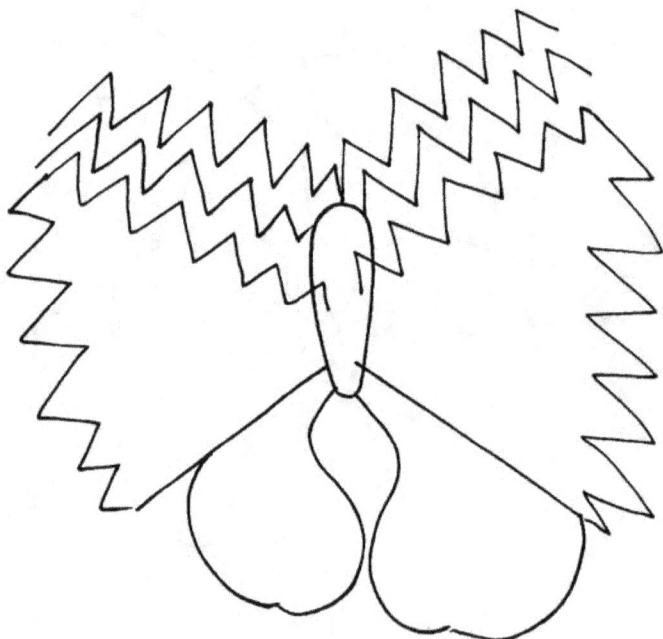

The Butterfly D

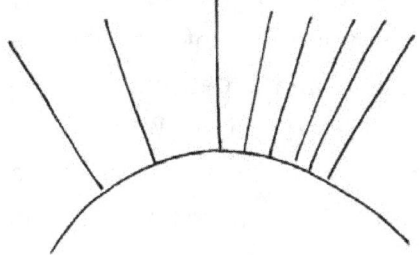

NeoWhimsies For Beginners: **10 NeoPopRealism Ink Drawing Projects**

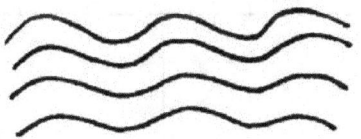

Draw the Mushrooms

𝒯he following pages will show you how to draw the NeoWhimsies mushrooms. Mushrooms typically look like umbrellas: they consist of a stalk topped by a cup-shaped or flat cap. Their spores are produced on special cells called basidia, located on the underside of the cap. Your drawing is a reflection of your mind. Through the line and repetitive patterns – ornaments – you are sharing your thoughts, you imagination. When you are stretching yourself beyond your limits, the practicing helps you to overcome any limitations that stand in the way of achieving the result. Have passion and confidence and you will be able to succeed. Be the best you can be, focus on your strengths, skills, and self-improvement. Turn your skills into the new strengths. When you draw NeoWhimsies mushrooms, you use your imagination. Each mushroom is different, however all of them created using the line and repetitive patterns. The visual instructions will lead you from the beginning to end of the drawing process. Every following image includes new detail(s). The final images look like this:

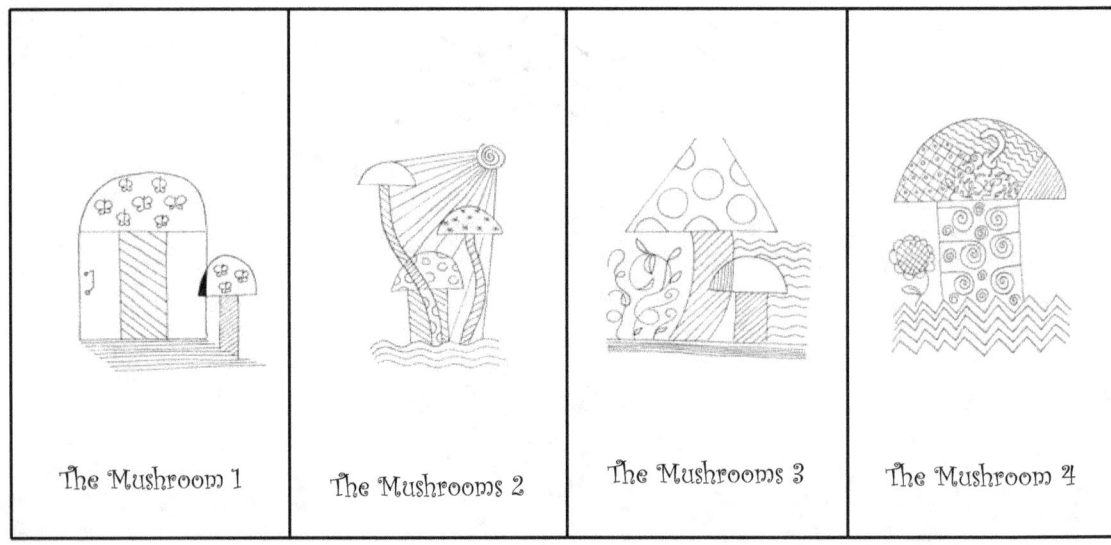

| The Mushroom 1 | The Mushrooms 2 | The Mushrooms 3 | The Mushroom 4 |

How to Draw Mushroom 1

This page includes the patterns used in NeoWhimsy Mushroom 1.

The Flies	The door handle
The door's strips	Stalk's strips
Strips	

Next pages contain the visual instructions that will show you step-by-step how to draw NeoWhimsy Mushroom 1.

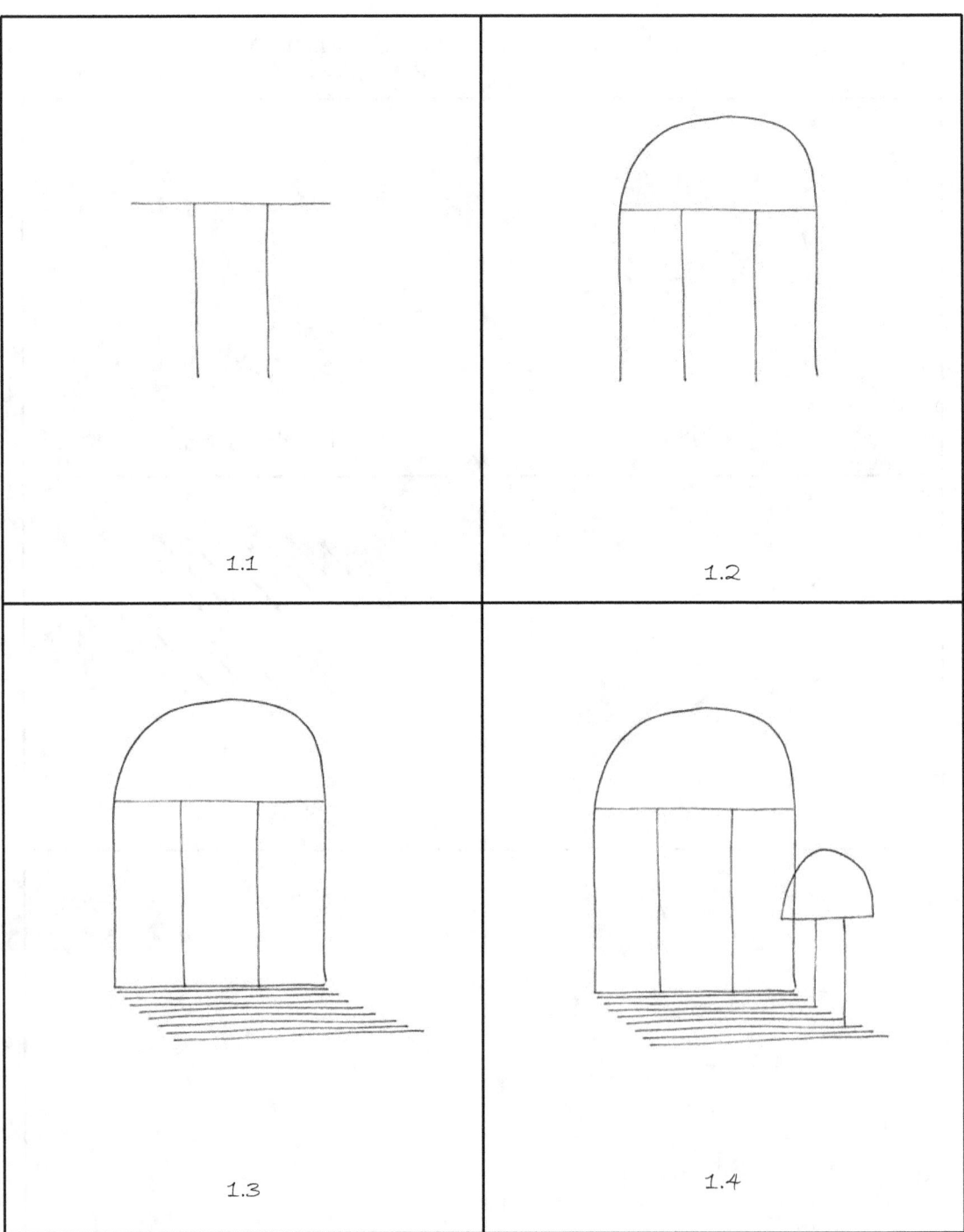

1.1

1.2

1.3

1.4

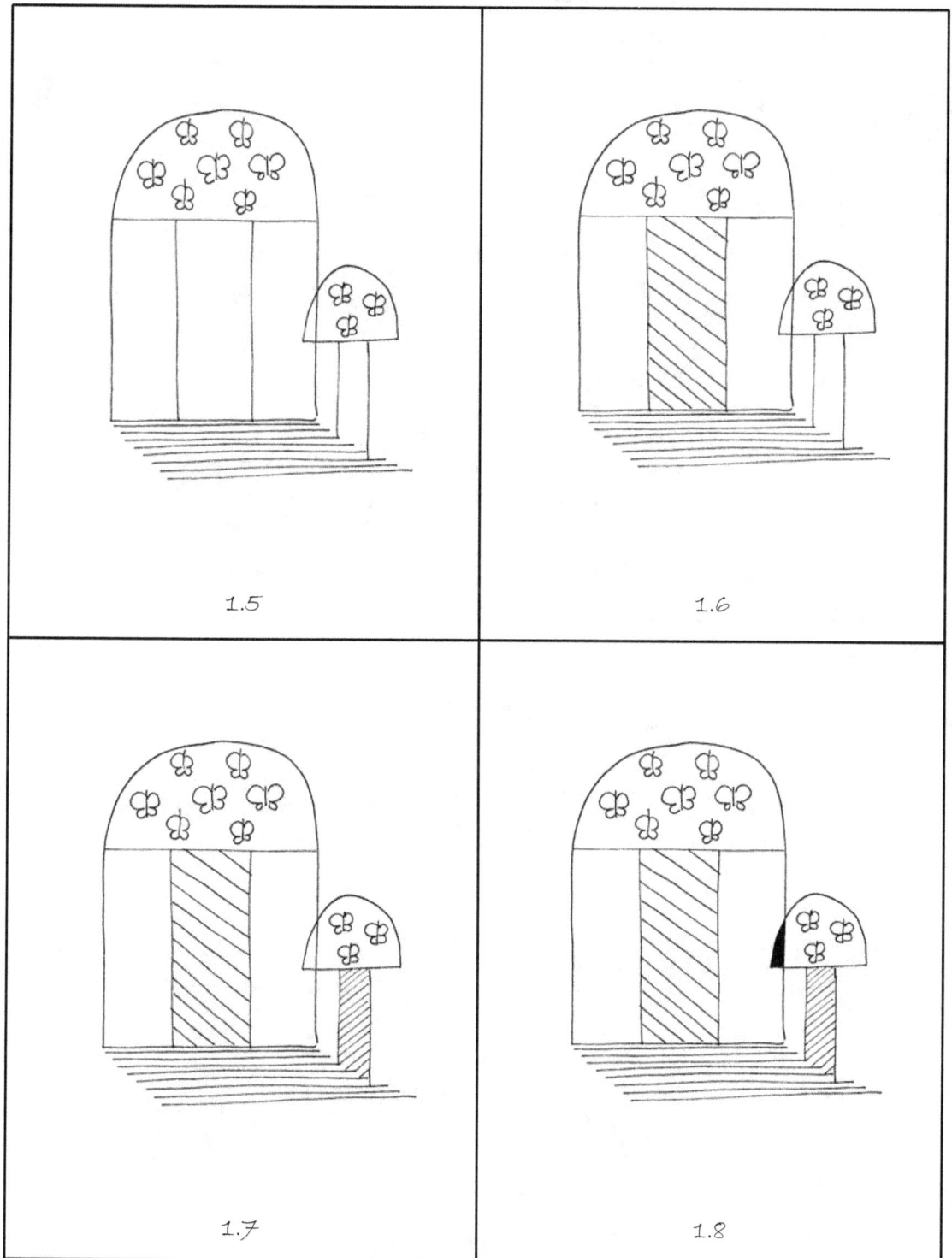

1.5

1.6

1.7

1.8

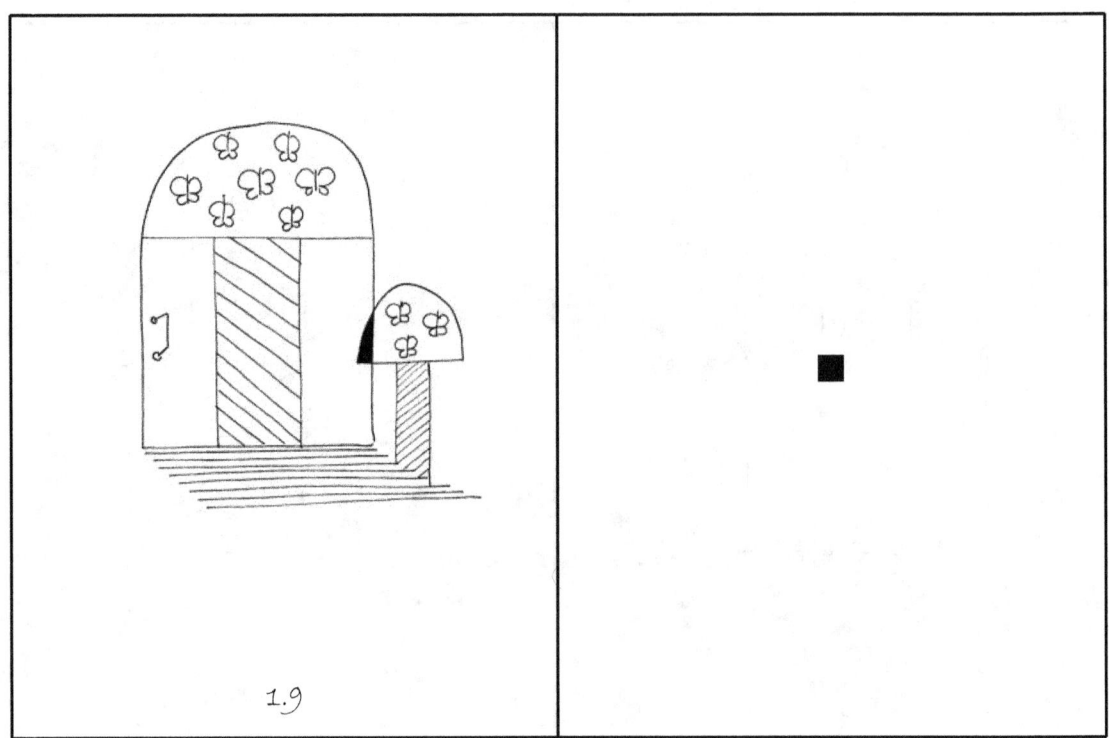

1.9

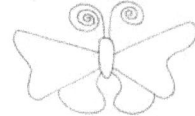

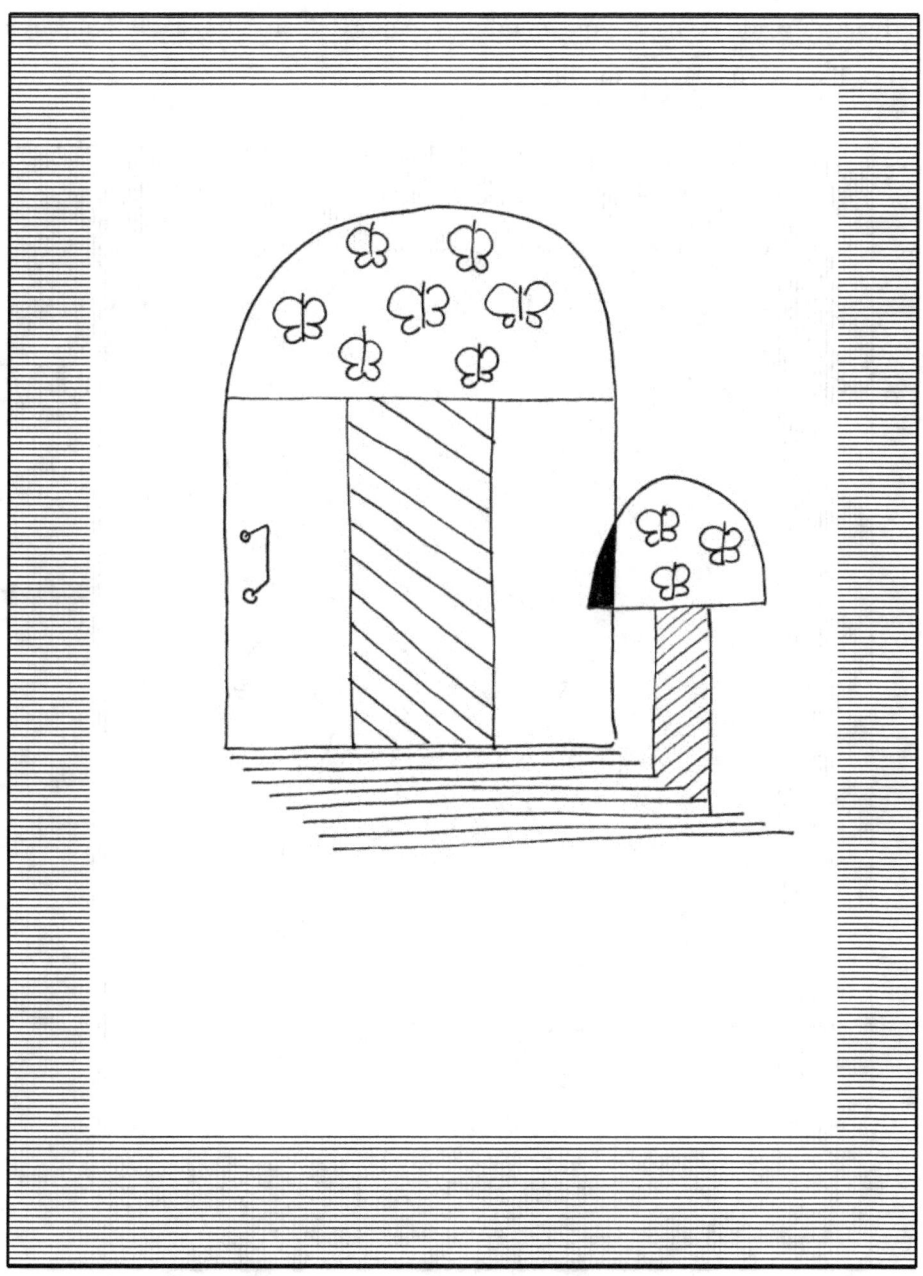

Serge E. Mikhailov, *The Mushroom 1*

How to Draw Mushrooms 2

Do not resist new ideas, open your mind and explore what is possible, employing your talent and skills. Learn, create, meditate!

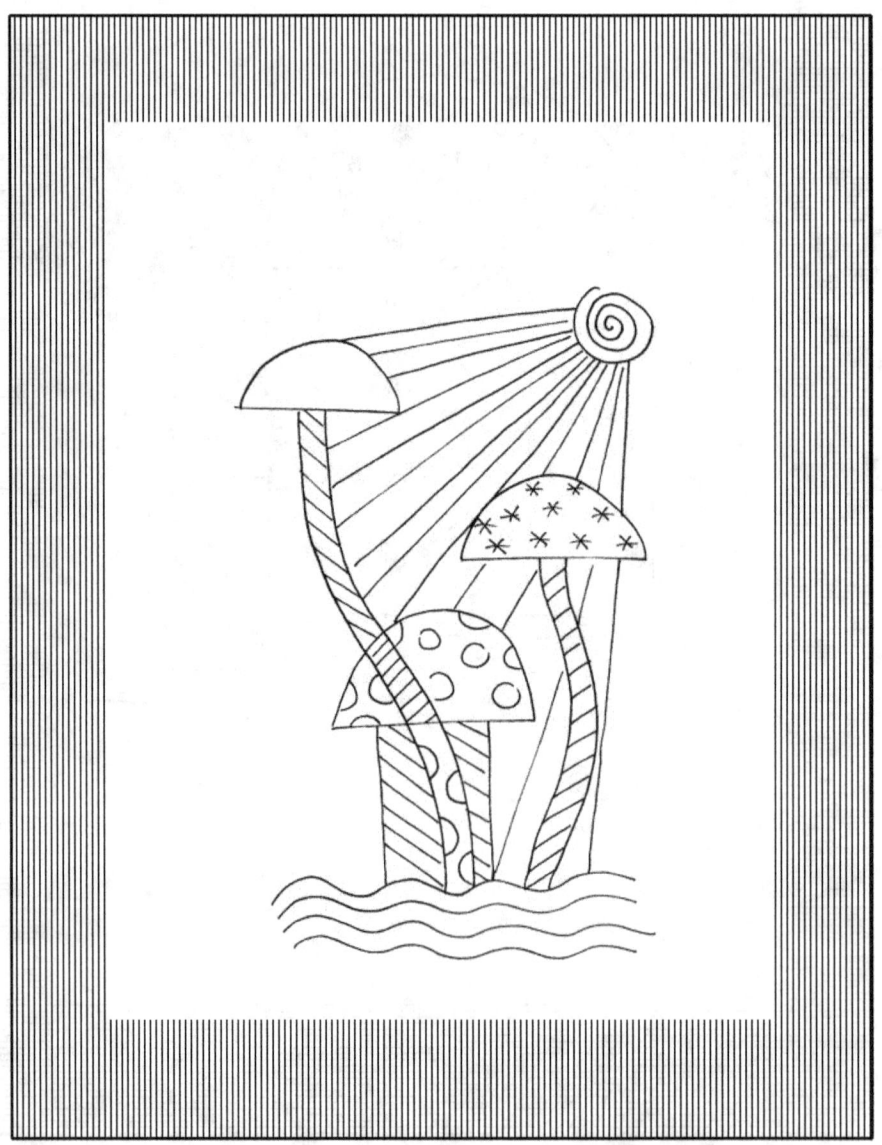

Serge E. Mikhailov, *The Mushrooms 2*

Learn about the repetitive patterns, which Serge E. Mikhailov used in NeoWhimsy Mushrooms 2.

Whirle	Rays strips	Stalk strips 1
Stalk strips 2	Stars	Circles
Waves		

Next pages contain the visual instructions, which will show you how to create NeoWhimsy Mushroom 2 step-by-step from the beginning to end. You will learn the process of the drawing. Practice and soon you will be able to draw your NeoWhimsies with ease, your line will flow freely and the compositions of your artworks will be more and more interesting and imaginative.

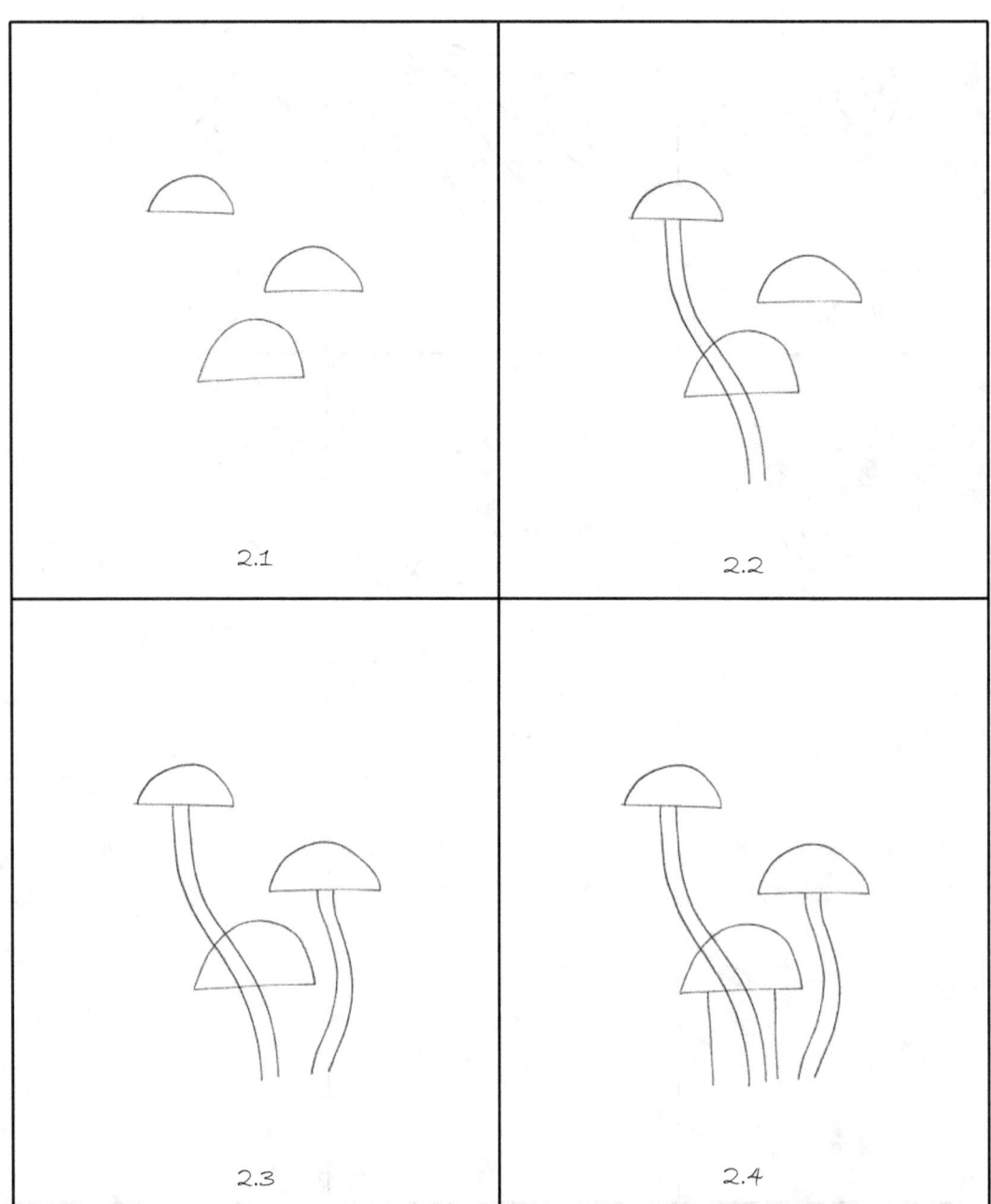

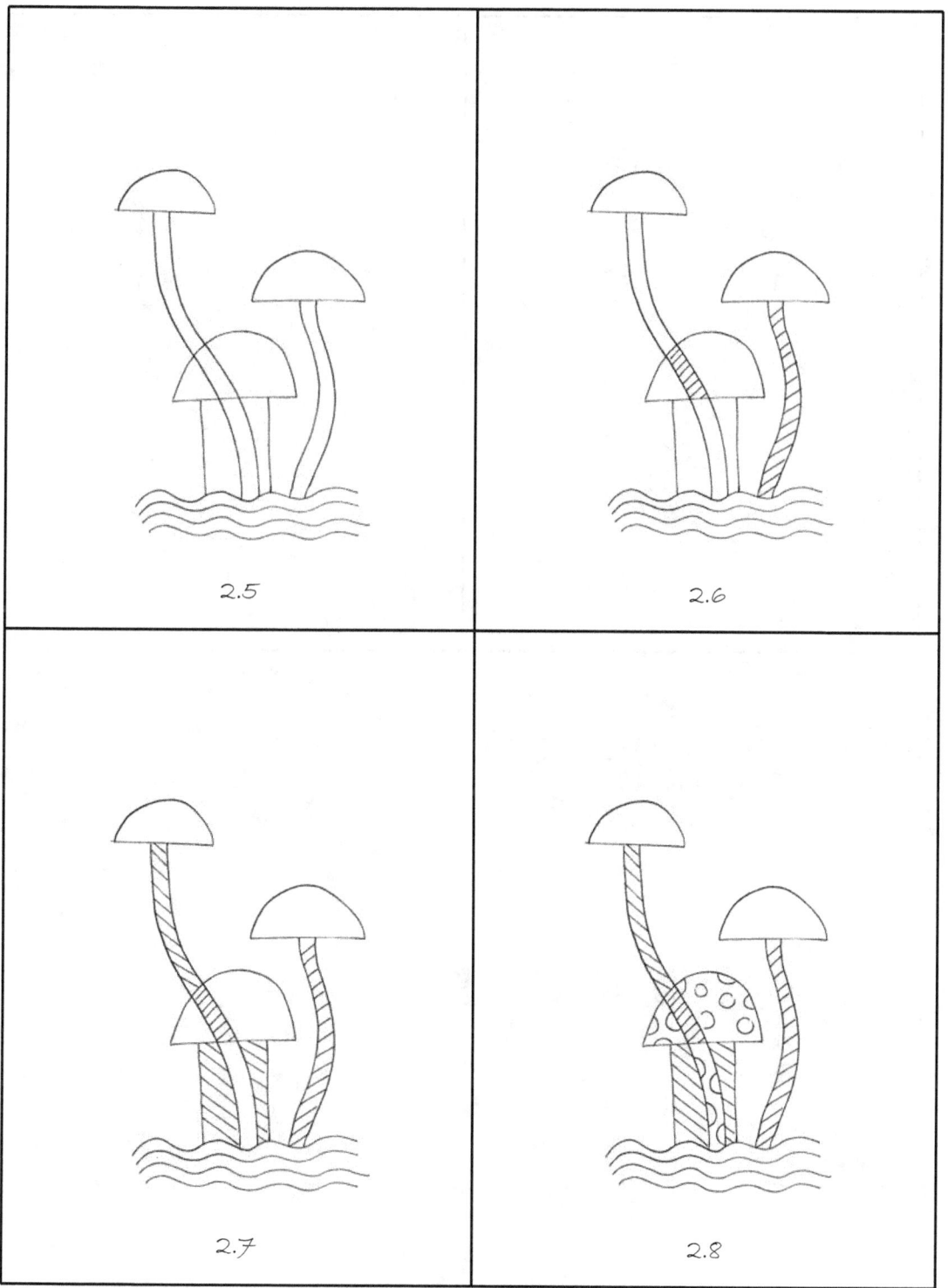

2.5

2.6

2.7

2.8

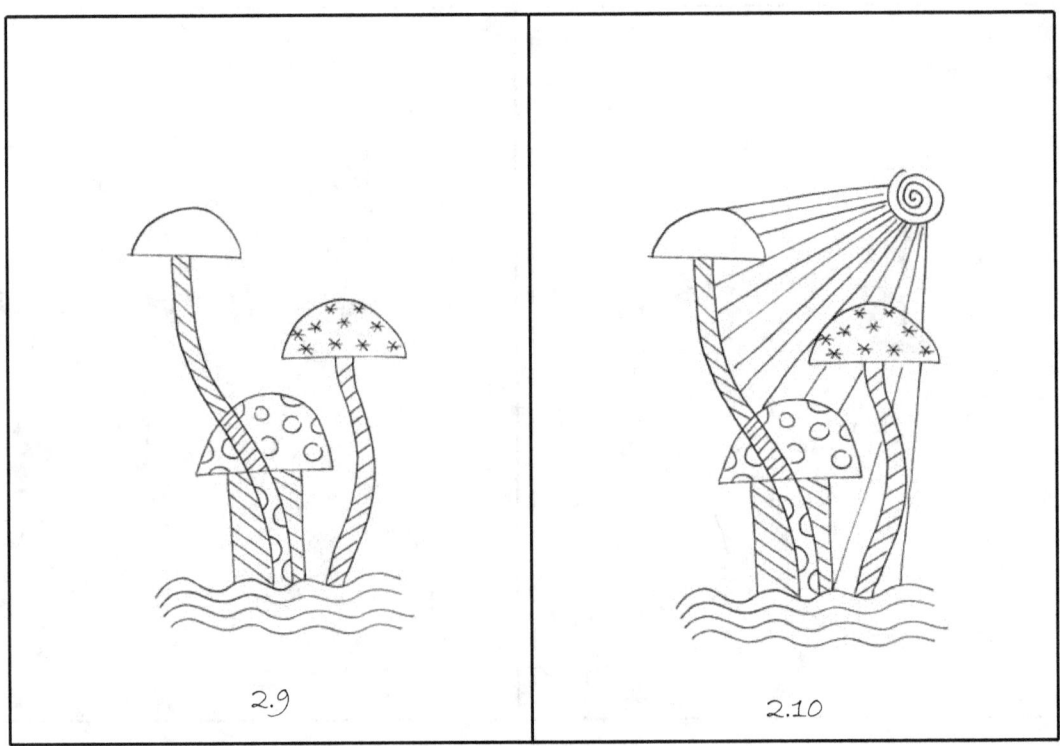

2.9   2.10

How to Draw Mushrooms 3

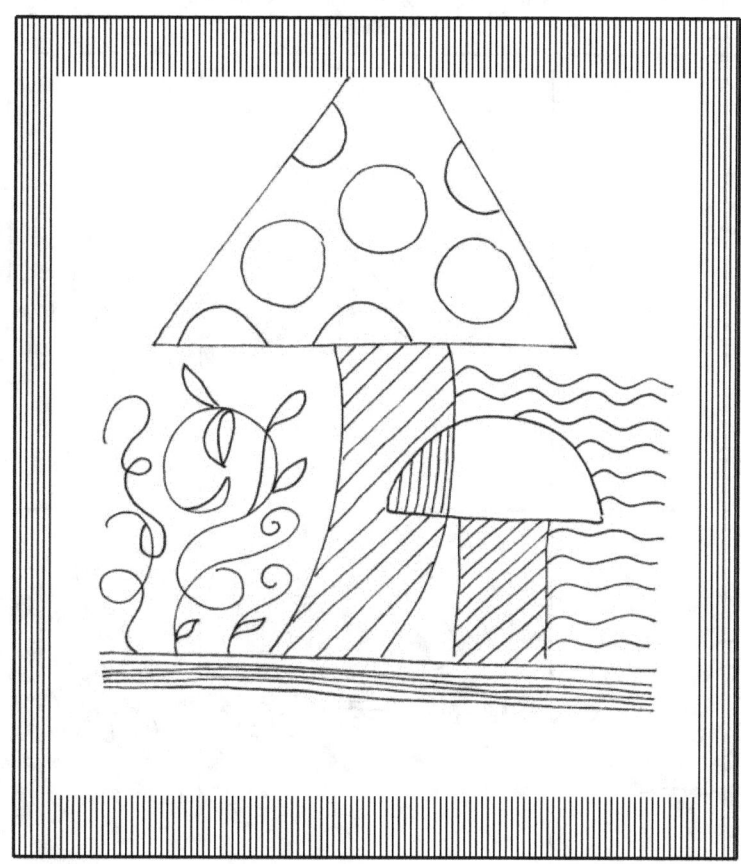

Serge E. Mikhailov, *The Mushrooms 3*

Next pages offer you the visual instructions, which show how to draw NeoWhimsy Mushrooms 3. Step-by-step, you will learn the developing process of a drawing from beginning to end. You will learn how to draw a line - a contour of mushrooms, and how to fill the sections with repetitive patterns - strips, circles, whirles, more. Learn to create the balanced and beautiful composition of a drawing. Drawings the combination of patterns is like playing jazz with its Syncopation. Syncopation is where the strong beat has been moved to a beat that is normally a weak beat. Practice and soon you will draw your NeoWhimsies with ease, your line will flow smooth and the compositions of your artworks will be more and more imaginative.

Learn how to draw the repetitive patterns used in NeoWhimsy Mushrooms *3*.

Circles	Stalk's strips	Cap's strips
Waves	Strips	Leaves
Whirles		

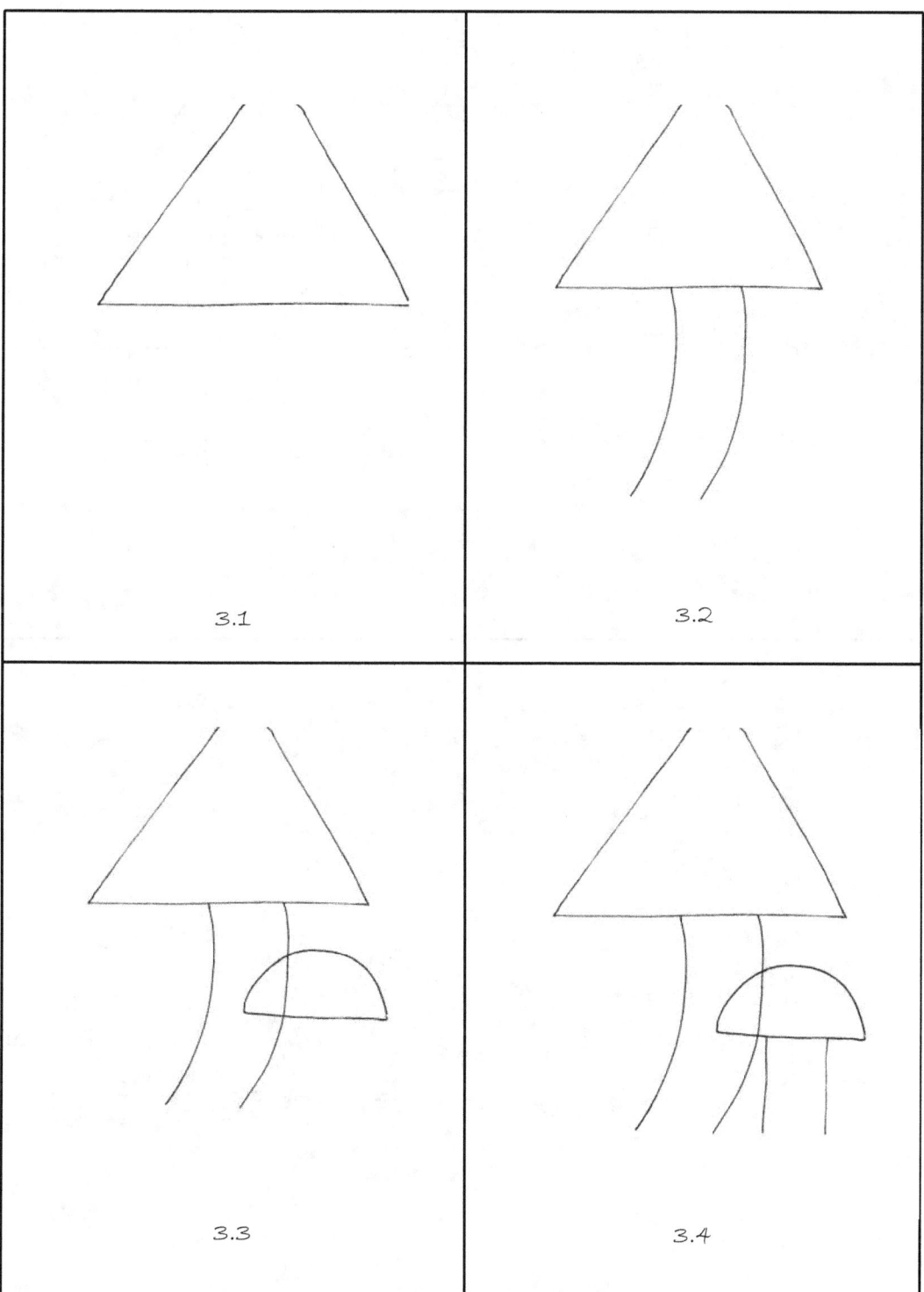

3.1

3.2

3.3

3.4

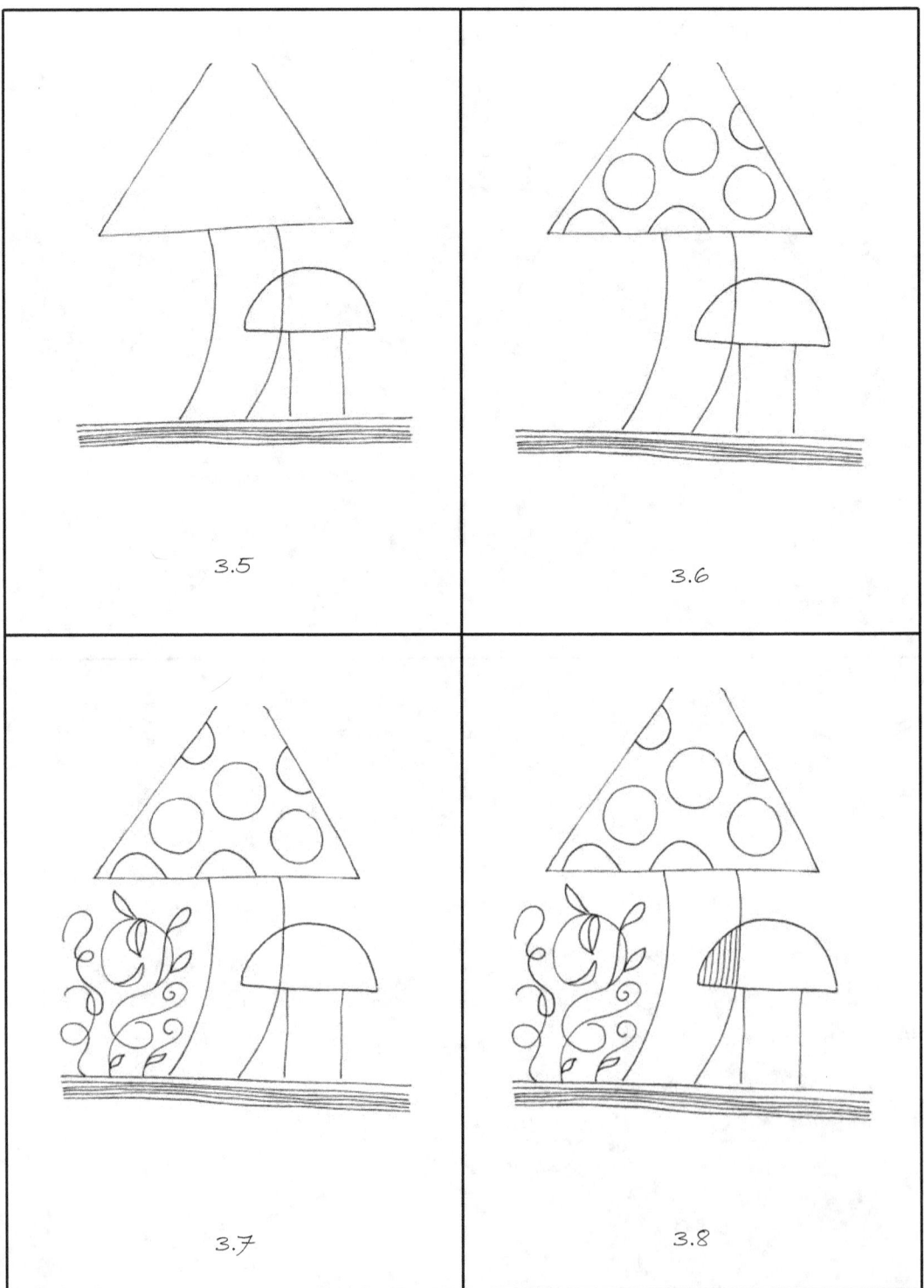

3.5

3.6

3.7

3.8

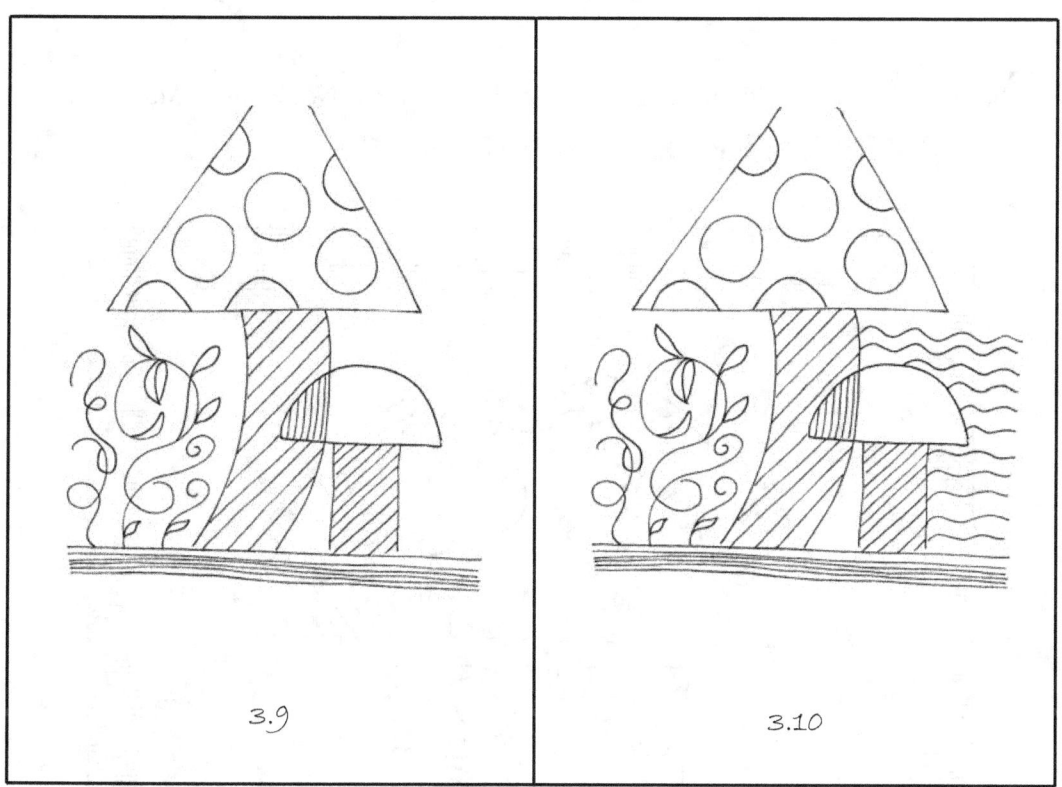

3.9   3.10

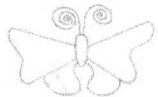

How to Draw Mushroom 4

The following pages will help you to learn how to draw NeoWhimsy Mushroom 4.

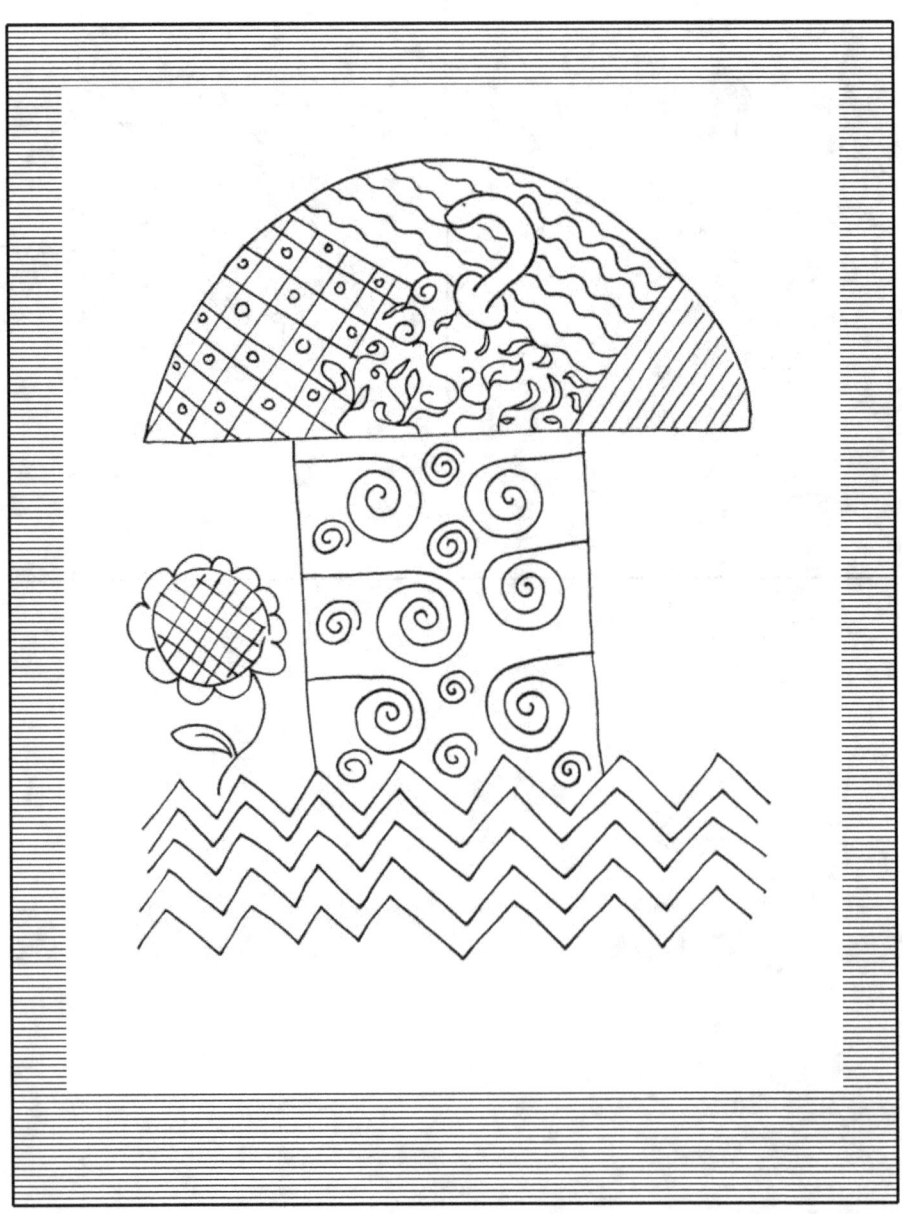

Serge E. Mikhailov, *The Mushroom 4*

The following patterns are used in NeoWhimsy Mushroom 4.

Squares and circles	Whirles	Double whirles
Leaves	Stalk big whirles	Zig–Zag
Flower		

The following pages include the visual instructions and show step–by–step how to draw NeoWhimsy Mushroom 4.

4.1

4.2

4.3

4.4

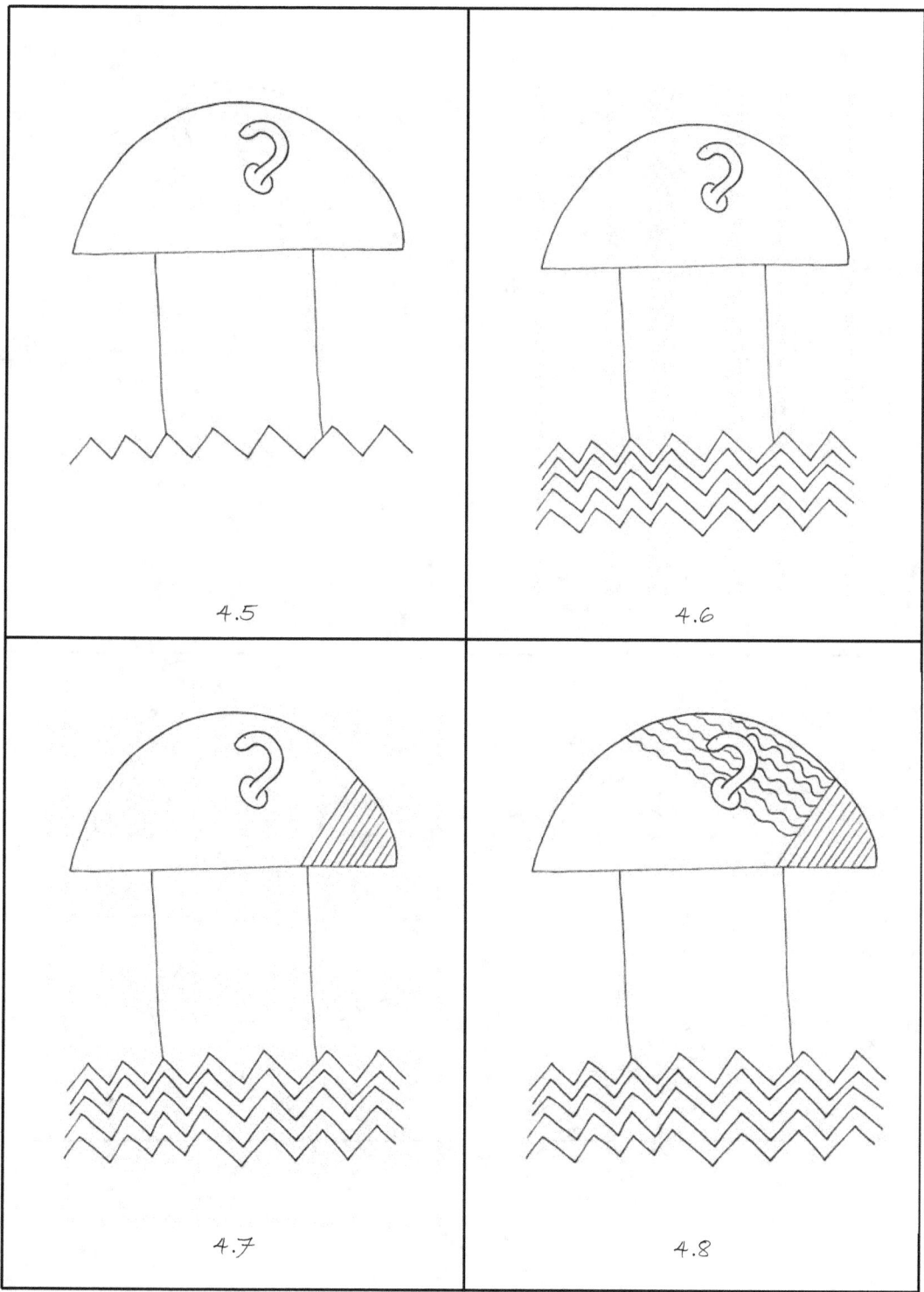

4.5

4.6

4.7

4.8

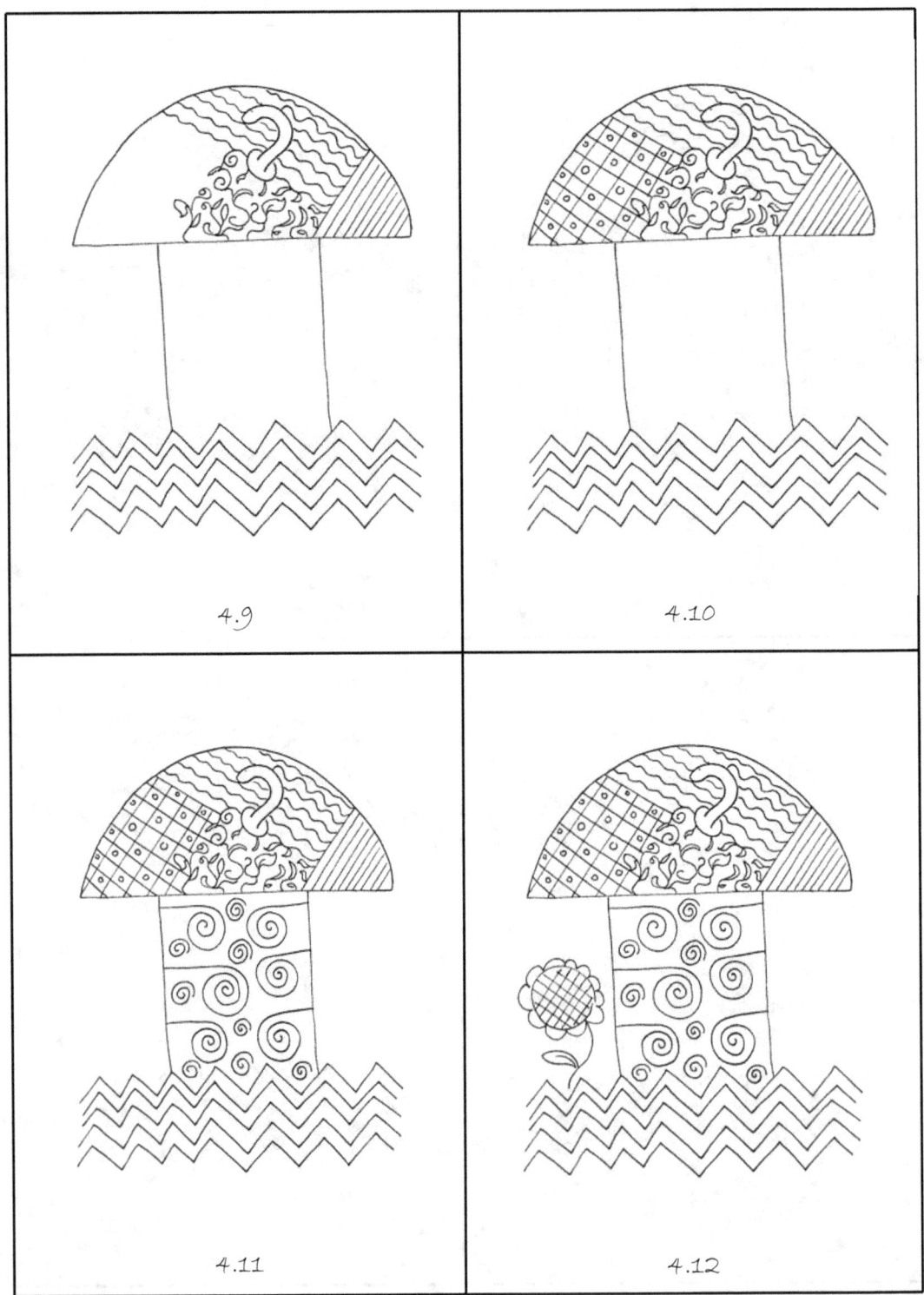

4.9

4.10

4.11

4.12

Draw the Mushrooms Here and Now

Serge has prepared for you more of the "skeletons", the base, and you should complete these artworks by putting some "meat" on the "bones" as you did before. Do not copy those NeoWhimsies that you see in this book, constantly create new and unique repetitive patterns. Use your imagination, employ your skill. Remember that imagination and inventiveness are necessary aspects of any creativity.

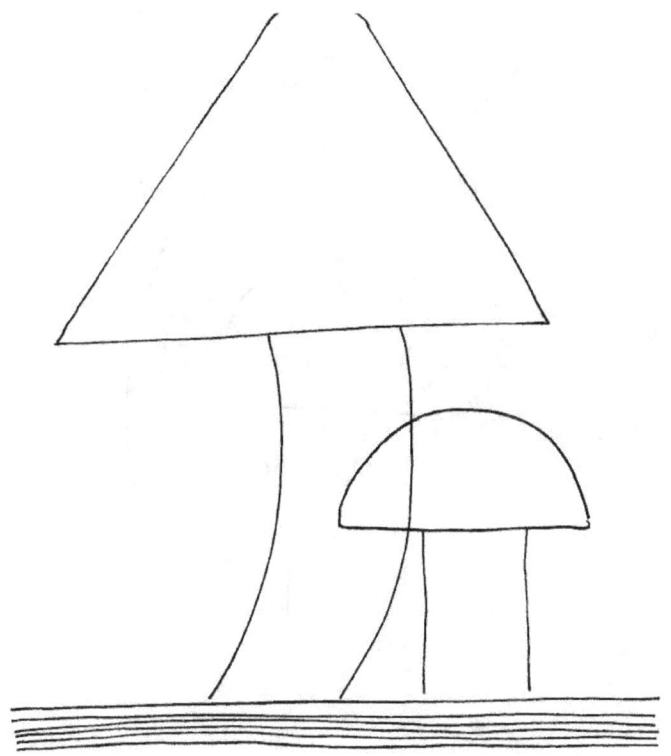

The Mushrooms A

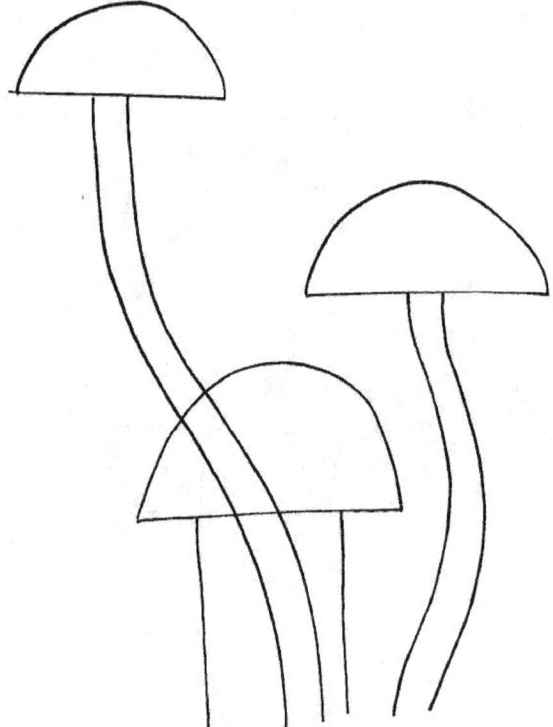

The Mushrooms B

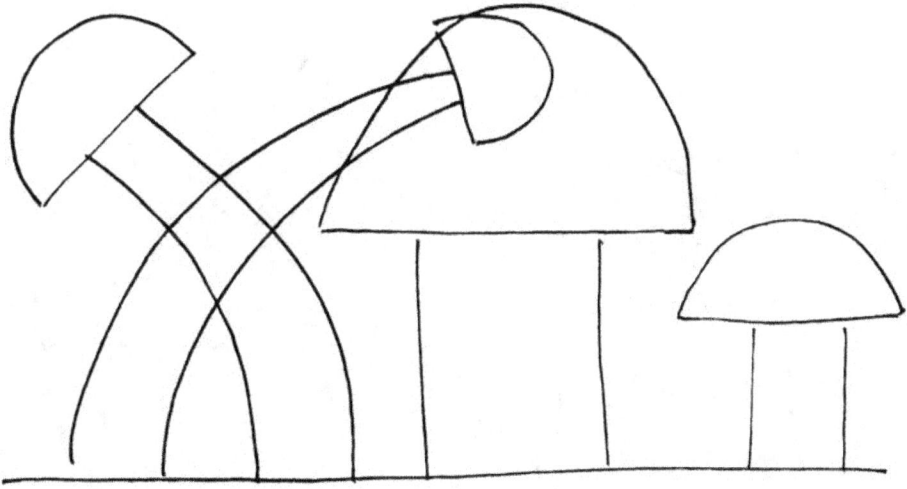

The Mushrooms C

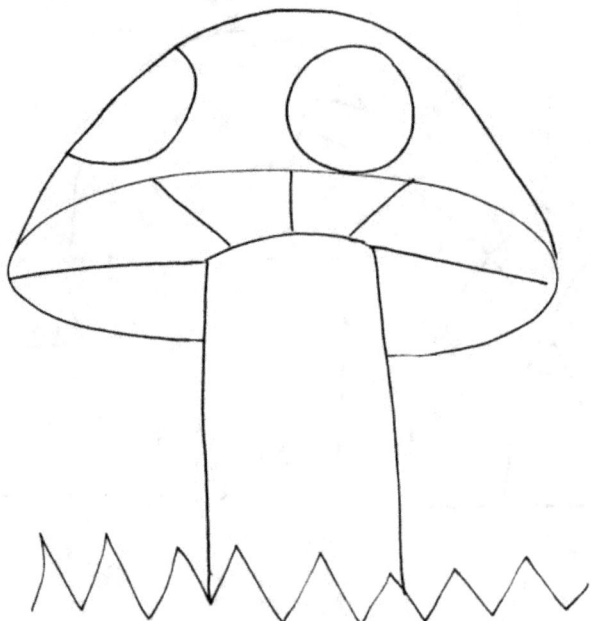

The Mushroom D

Create Your NeoWhimsies from the Scratch

Use the following pages to create new NeoWhimsies. Draw the imaginative mushrooms, snakes, cocks with beautiful tails and fanciful-looking sea fishes, anything you like. Draw a flowing line that creates the sections. Then, fill the sections, which appeared, with different repetitive patterns – imaginative ornaments. Use the circle, squares, triangles, rectangular, dots, rays, strips, "snakes", small flowers, other objects, their combinations in different variations, combine different sizes. Some sections leave blank. Use your imagination and artistic intuition, develop your skills. Draw your NeoWhimsies step-by-step as you learned from this book. When you draw, relax and you will enter the meditative state of mind. More you draw, the better your drawings are. Have fun, create, meditate!

Draw your NeoWhimsy here. Create, have fun, meditate!

Draw your NeoWhimsy here. Create, have fun, meditate!

Create Your Repetitive Patterns *Gallery*

$\mathscr{U}$se the following pages to create the repetitive patterns Gallery. Fill each section with the different imaginative ornaments – repetitive patterns. To create your patterns use the line, circles, squares, triangles, zig–zags, rectangular, rays, "snakes", dots, small flowers, other small objects, anything your imagination tells you. You will use these patterns later in your future NeoWhimsies drawings. Remember that human's imagination is unlimited and impossible is nothing. Practice, develop your skills, have fun!

1	2	3
4	5	6
7	8	9

10	11	12
13	14	15
16	17	18
19	20	21

From illustrator Serge E. Mikhailov

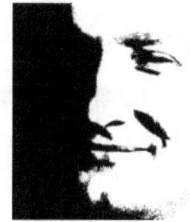

Hello, my name is Serge E. Mikhailov. I like to draw in graphic style! And I hope you too! I would like to say thank you to the NeoPopRealism PRESS for cooperation and the new ideas.

I was born in 1970 in Russia, in the City of Khabarovsk, located 19 miles from the Chinese border. In 1998, I began to draw and was influenced by Picasso and Matisse. I authored a book on the self improvement and imagination and now involved in a few Internet projects that help people develop their imagination and the drawing skills (http://hohou.com).

When I found out about the NeoPopReaism ink drawing style, I thought it is unusual and fun to use the ornamental patterns in the drawing. It was something new to me. The ornament – the patterns – carry the extra emotions and information, the subconscious emotions. This type of drawing is able to hide the inaccuracy and a person can draw without eraser. The NeoPopRealism ink images look complete.

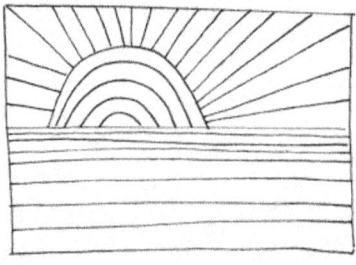

Take a look at a simple picture of the sunset on the left. This drawing is complete and it uses the patterns of NeoPopRealism. Everyone can draw in the NeoPopRealism style!

I ride my bicycle, take photos and draw to relax. When a person draws, he/she uses the sub-consciousness, trying to connect the different concepts in his/her mind. The drawing is a meditative process (trance). If you would like to know what is on your mind, then draw! When you are relaxed, you can draw the wide pictures. When you are full of energy, then you draw the zigzags (ornament). Turn the pictures and you will see the different emotions. If you would like to learn how to draw, I would be happy to teach you!

Conclusion

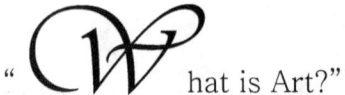 " hat is Art?"

Now, when you learned how to draw the NeoPopRealism ink images – the NeoWhimsies, you might have your answer to this open question. We'd like to hear from you, e-mail us neopoprealismpress@mail.com. Also, if you have a blog, post there the images of your NeoPopRealism ink drawings and a story about how you learned to draw them. And, please, mention there this book with NeoPopRealism creator Nadia Russ. Have a wonderful journey to the world of NeoPopRealism!

NeoPopRealism ten canons for happier life:

1. Be beautiful.

2. Be creative and productive; never stop studying and learning.

3. Be peace-loving, positive-minded.

4. Do not accept totalitarian philosophy.

5. Be free-minded, do the best you can to move the world to peace and harmony.

6. Be family oriented, self-disciplined.

7. Be free spirited. Follow your dreams, if they are not destructive, but constructive.

8. Believe in GOD. God is one. It is harmony and striving for perfection.

9. Be supportive to those who need you, be generous.

10. Create your life as a great adventurous story.

Nadia Russ, 2004

Additional books – teaching / learning material on NeoPopRealism Ink drawing for adults, teenagers and children

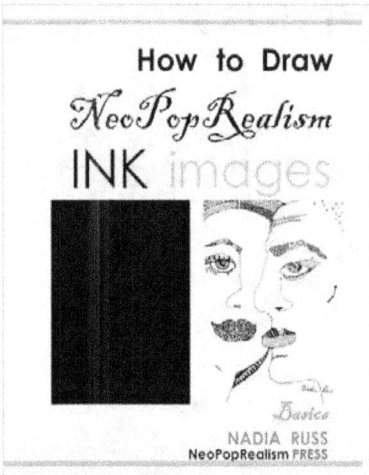

ISBN: 9780615515755
FOR TEENS & ADULTS

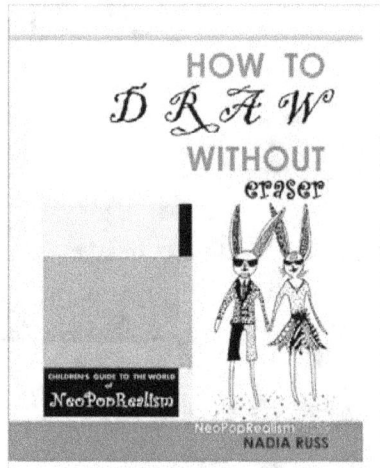

ISBN: 9780615521824
FOR CHILDREN

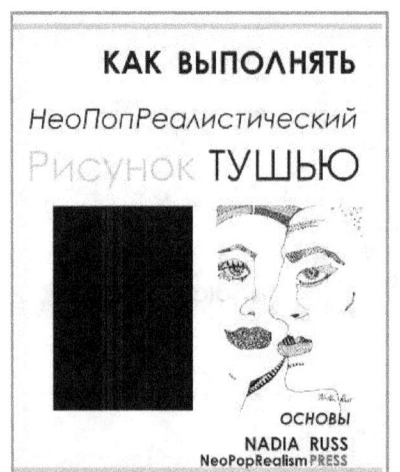

Book *"How to Draw NeoPopRealism Ink Images: Basics"* in Russian translation.
ISBN: 9780615516967

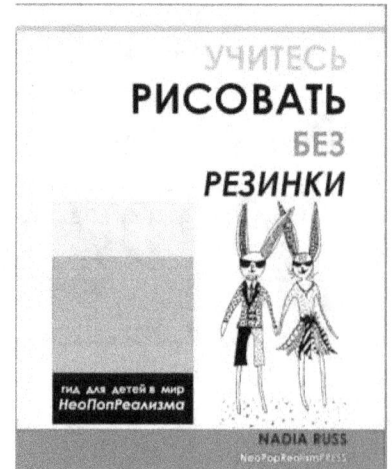

Book *"How to Draw Without Eraser: Backgrounds"* in Russian translation.
ISBN: 9780615523484

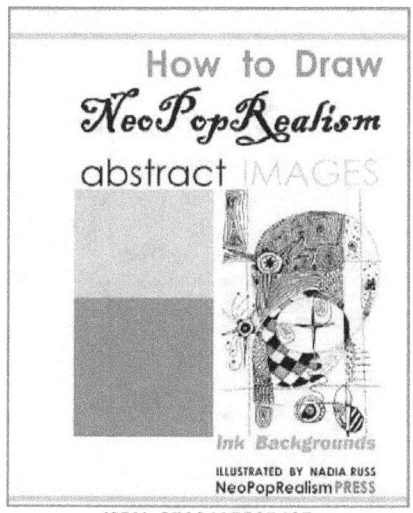

ISBN: 9780615527437
FOR TEENS & ADULTS

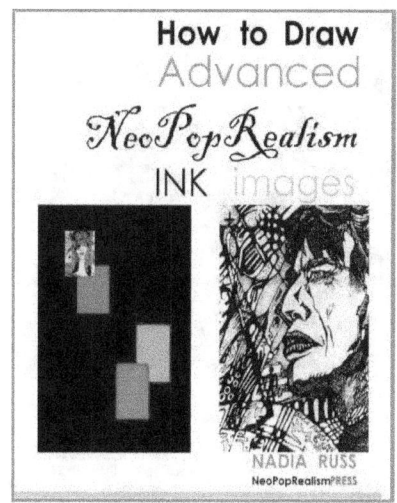

ISBN: 9780615569758
FOR TEENS & ADULTS

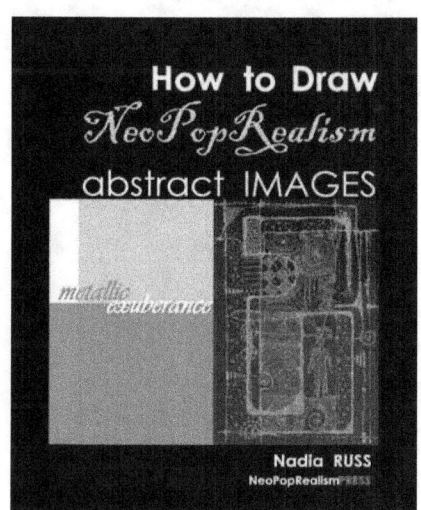

ISBN: 9780615560991
FOR TEENS & ADULTS

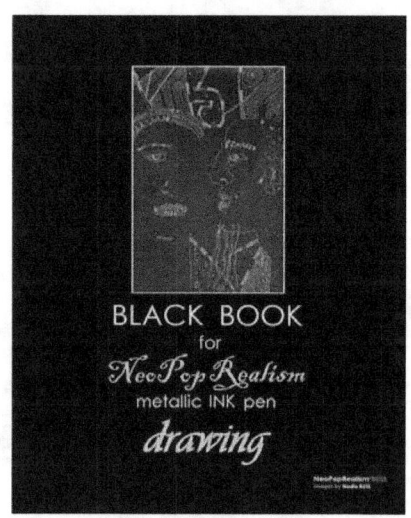

ISBN:9780615561028
FOR ALL AGES & LEVELS

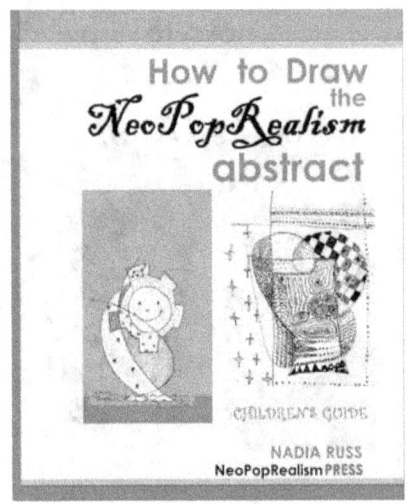

ISBN: 9780615545332
FOR CHILDREN

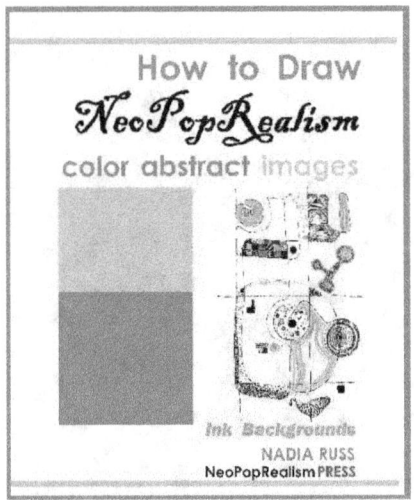

ISBN: 9780615579559
FOR TEENS & ADUTS

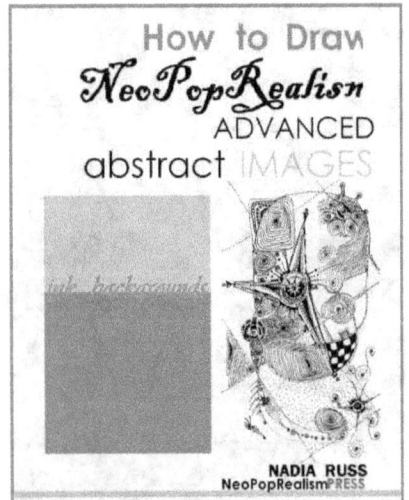

ISBN: 9780615592558
FOR TEENS & ADULTS

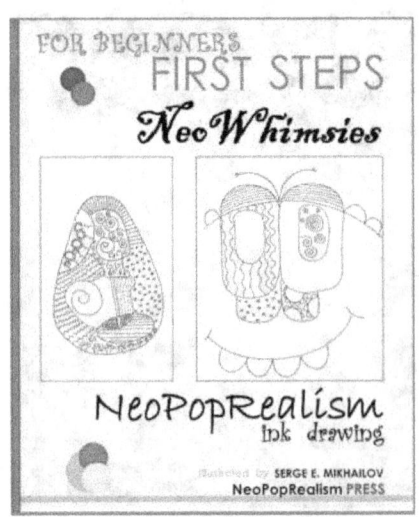

ISBN: 9780615641553
FOR CHILDREN & ARTISANS

www.ingramcontent.com/pod-product-compliance
Lightning Source LLC
Chambersburg PA
CBHW081206180526
45170CB00006B/2229